Ham and Pete
in wartii

LEONARD CHAVE
J. M. LEE

RICHMOND LOCAL HISTORY SOCIETY
2011

Other books in this series:
Kew at War
Richmond at war (in preparation)

© Richmond Local History Society 2011

ISBN 978-0-9550717-6-8

Printed and bound in Great Britain by the Doppler Press, 5 Wates Way,
Brentwood, Essex CM15 9TB

Editorial note

Following the successful publication of *Kew at War* in 2009, Richmond Local History Society decided that two further volumes should be prepared, covering the same period in Ham/Petersham and Richmond itself. But how was our village to match the drama of the US Topographical army and the colourful Italian prisoners-of-war who succeeded them?

We did have our own wartime secrets on a national scale, with the establishment of RADAR research and the interrogation centre at Latchmere House, and these have provided substantial parts of this book. There was only one person capable of writing on the former, and a recent release of information after 50 years provided much valuable and accurate information for the second.

Professor Lee has written on the RADAR topic for *Richmond History 28* and given subsequent expanded talks on the subject. But his professional knowledge has also laid a foundation for chapters giving the background against which civilian Britain entered into war. He encouraged me to research and to write up the last days of Ham as an independent Council in *Richmond History 26* and 27, so we have worked together again harmoniously on this book, collecting and exchanging information relevant to each other's contributions; we hope the result is not a monstrous hybrid, but rather another step in literary evolution.

So why not *Ham and Petersham at War*? We never were in that state with each other, but cooperated in various ways during 1939/1945; the story is thus of recent victims of a shotgun wedding learning to live together in concord and making the best of difficult times.

Leonard Chave

A NOTE ON PRICES

All prices quoted are in pre-decimal sterling, where $2\frac{1}{2}d = 1$ new penny, and 1 *shilling* = 5 new pence. To compare with current values, it is necessary to multiply by about x50.

Contents

Introduction

The emergencies of the Second World War brought Ham and Petersham together as part of the borough of Richmond in ways not envisaged when the boundaries were redrawn in 1933. The boundary changes were part of a general government policy to abolish small local authorities. Ham Urban District Council was dissolved and the greater part of its jurisdiction was taken into Richmond. It looks as if the constraints of wartime life and the general mood of the 'People's War' led the local authority to contemplate improvements that might come from a better system of town and country planning. The effects of the War on this revision of boundaries perhaps still linger on.

The expansion of the area under the control of Richmond Council was dramatic. The acreage that came under its administration and bye-laws was increased by almost 40 per cent. Ham and Petersham were brought together to form a new polling district, the Sudbrook Ward, the largest in the borough with the smallest population, electing three councillors, one of whom retired each year. They adopted a Richmond custom started by the Kew Society in 1900 of establishing a ratepayers' association that could avoid the expense of a contested election by nominating a councillor who would not be opposed. Before 1933 Petersham had been part of the South Ward of Richmond without any representation of its own. Wanting to elect three councillors outright and annoyed by the rule that there had to be only one vacancy a year, the association was proposed by Petersham Vestry and by some Ham residents who called a meeting in Trefoil House, Petersham, in October 1933. It was successful initially in reducing the number of contests. Their first unopposed representative was Alfred Allum, an estate steward living in Bute Lodge. But from 1935 onwards the Labour Party started to challenge the independents on a regular basis, though without success.

The new suburb at its beginning was almost entirely rural. Ham Urban District Council had managed the farming landscape that lay between Richmond Park and the Thames and between the truly urban centres of Kingston-upon-Thames and Richmond. The dominant feature of the district was the estate of the Earls of Dysart, the Tollemache family, who owned Ham House. The presence of that family kept local agriculture in being, and the 1902 Act of Parliament, which placed restrictions on housing development in order to preserve the view from Richmond Hill, endowed Petersham, in particular, with the special status of looking attractive for the public good.

There had been a precedent for taking open ground into the borough. Petersham had been incorporated in 1892 in order to deal with the anomaly of an ancient ecclesiastical parish that included Kew. But on that occasion urban development had been limited. The mayor, Sir Whittaker Ellis, bought Bute House in Petersham in the expectation he would be able to profit from the construction of a number of private villas in its grounds. Having demolished the house, he found himself caught up in the campaign to preserve the view from Richmond Hill, and he sold the property to Mrs. Letitia Warde of Petersham Lodge, who made clear that her purchase was a contribution to that campaign. The latter also kept Petersham meadow in its pastoral state. Petersham with 150–160 private houses retained its village character and rural setting.

In 1933 both Richmond and Kingston were looking for land on which to build local authority housing. In that year the borough had just come to terms with a major change in its own urban structure. The opening of the Great Chertsey Road and of Twickenham Bridge to carry it across the river had required the demolition of many working-class houses on the line of the new road and near the gas works. Several local businesses had been forced to move. The road had taken away the intimacy of links between the Green and the Old Deer Park. It looked as if the Council would have to make a special effort to help the dispossessed.

Bringing Ham into the borough was the outcome of long arguments about the implementation of the Local Government Act of 1929. Under that legislation Surrey County Council was obliged to revise its internal boundaries. Ham had to be divided or to join either Kingston or Richmond. Middlesex similarly on the other side of the Thames considered how to move Teddington, Hampton and Hampton Wick into the borough of Twickenham by the same legislation. The first proposal was that the whole of Ham should join Kingston. For many in Ham there seemed to be closer ties with the borough on its southern side both in local services and in opportunities for employment. The Leyland works provided jobs. Nothing was decided before the National Census of 1931 which included supplements on the boundary changes that had already been agreed.

The final settlement gave to Richmond by far the largest part of what had been Ham Urban District. Kingston acquired 251 acres (13.5%) but Richmond 1,869 acres (86.5%). The failure to determine a boundary before the 1931 Census makes it difficult to provide accurate figures for the division of the population. The population of the UDC in the Census was 2,206. It looks as if 727 (33%) became residents of Kingston but 1,479 (67%) those of Richmond.

The new suburb to emerge from this settlement can be studied in at least three stages. First, for six years (1933–39) in a fairly piecemeal fashion Richmond Council sought to bring both council housing and private estate development to Ham, often facing difficulties generated by the trustees of the Ham House estate. There was a massive increase in population which seemed to threaten its rural character. The population of Ham was about four times that of what it had been in 1931. Second, during six years of war (1939–45) there was a strong contrast in the patterns of property requisition for war purposes between Petersham and Ham. Third, in the post-war years the area was influenced by ideas of town and country planning and of social reconstruction in planning for the future. This book covers the second stage.

At the outbreak of war Ham was a very different place from its appearance under its former urban district council. 272 local authority houses and 157 for sale to private buyers had been completed, although there were still three farms in Ham and one in Petersham left untouched, plus green spaces earmarked as Green Belt Land or for further planned development for housing and recreation. The Ham River Grit Company had done much excavation in land adjoining the Thames; most of the roads that now branch off from the present A307 came to an end at the edge of the gravel workings. Only the main road, Ham Gate Avenue (when the Park was open) and Tudor Drive gave access to adjoining districts. Two road bridges that appear in the 1913 Ham town plan had not been built, so between Kingston and Richmond only the Teddington footbridge and two ferries gave pedestrian access to the north bank of the Thames.

Richmond's housing developments had covered most of the ground between Ham Street (the oldest street in Ham) and the gravel pits. One school (now the Catholic Church) existed in Ham, and the Russell School in Petersham Park, but for secondary education it was necessary for children to travel into Richmond, using the 65 or 73 bus as their only public transport link. Car ownership was very rare at that time. There was the ancient church of St Peter with the village hall next to the sister church of All Saints', the Ham parish church of St Andrew and an Evangelical church in Lock Road: Catholic education and worship were only available in Richmond.

There was nevertheless still evidence of the constraints on rural society imposed by landowners. The 9th Earl of Dysart, although blind and disabled, had been in residence at Ham House until his death in 1935. Sir Lyonel Tollemache, who inherited the baronetcy but not the peerage, succeeded him as the local squire; he lived in Ham throughout the war. Control of the family's land was vested in Buckminster Estates in 1934, the year before the Earl's death and the passing of the title to his niece in Scotland. Twice during the late 1930s developments in Ham proposed by Richmond Council were blocked by disagreements with Buckminster, the first having potentially severe defects during wartime. A proposal to erect a fire station in Ham Street with a Mother and Child clinic and a decontamination centre was turned down, and when later an alternative development was proposed, linking the proposed clinic with a branch library, reading room, community hall and cultural centre, it was also rejected on the grounds that it might create disturbance to the residents of the Tollemache Almshouses opposite (though the library would have been accepted). Ham could have been classed as an area severely deprived of social amenities, given the actual and potential growth in population. A further indication of lack of freedom for development was the fact that so many houses were leased from Buckminster rather than owned as freehold. When the sale of 350 acres of Dysart land took place by auction in 1949, the leases of as many as 140 properties were included.

The character of Richmond's new suburb was beginning to take shape. The electors of Sudbrook Ward during the war had to rely on three independent councillors for the representation of their views on local issues. The government suspended elections for the duration of hostilities. The constraints of war on everyday life helped Ham and Petersham to come to terms with the effects of the 1933 settlement. All the regulations and the appeals for voluntary labour came from Richmond town hall.

CHAPTER ONE

The constraints of war on everyday life

The outbreak of war placed everybody under regulations that touched upon nearly all aspects of civilian life. Parliament passed the Emergency Powers Act which allowed the government to rule by decree. Some restrictions had been planned well in advance of events; others were innovations to meet the conditions of the moment. Civil servants in secret had set up plans and designated personnel for those ministerial departments that needed to have war functions only, such as the Ministry of Supply and the Ministry of Information.

The Home Office was in advance of all others in the preparation of 'air raid precautions' (ARP). The volunteers trained to assist the evacuation of women and children from London and other towns had already been given opportunities to practice in 1938–9 after the Munich crisis when Neville Chamberlain, as prime minister, attempted to negotiate with Hitler. The enemy was expected to bomb cities from the air, and perhaps use gas. Air raid shelters and gasmasks were distributed in anticipation of hostilities. But those recruited into the 'local defence volunteers' (LDV) – later called the Home Guard in 1940 – had no such initiations. The special forces called Auxiliary Units which would lead the resistance to enemy occupation had even less. They both had to face the prospect of a German invasion in September 1940 without adequate arms or a proper preparation for the tasks ahead. Nobody had anticipated the speed with which the British Expeditionary Force in Europe would be forced to retreat and to evacuate from Dunkirk or with which the French would be compelled to surrender. The events of May 1940 marked the end of what came to be called 'the Phoney War' – the period from September 1939 during which the dispersal of people and national treasures from the places in which they were concentrated seemed unnecessary, because the bombing that had been expected was not in evidence. Civilians on 'the Home Front' were kept in waiting for the trials of the 'blitz' – the German strategy used on the Continent of a sudden and intensive aerial attack or 'blitzkrieg'. The Air Ministry thought that 'the Battle of Britain' ran from 8 August to 31 October 1940.

The most immediate effect of war on daily life was the blackout – fitting shutters or other coverings to all windows to prevent light leaving a building at night, an elementary air raid precaution. Daylight hours were also used more efficiently by changing the setting between local time and Greenwich Mean Time (GMT). Summer Time (GMT+1) was brought forward in February 1940, and the whole country moved to Double Summer Time (GMT+2) in 1941.

Another obvious cause for concern was the obligation to register for both military service and food rationing. Everyone was required to have an identity card with a 7 or 8 digit number and to carry a ration book filled with coupons which were handed to the retailer with whom the family was registered. Grocers and other tradesmen could only replace the stock in their shops by surrendering such coupons to their regular suppliers. Each individual had a flat-rate ration. There were no special allocations for labourers or growing boys. The Ministry of Food was created as soon as war was declared to administer the system and to give advice on diet; each local authority had a local food control committee. The schemes for registration and food rationing proceeded at a reasonable pace and with few problems because they had both been designed and tested from 1936 onwards.

The principal grocers in Ham and Petersham were Chinnerys in Petersham Road and David Fieldson in Ham Street. The local office of the Ministry of Labour & National Service, where men received their call-up papers, was in Onslow Hall on Little Green in Richmond, next to the Richmond Theatre.

The National Register was the basis of the scheme for conscripting men into military service. Parliament passed the National Service (Armed Forces) Act which set in motion the 'call-up' of each generation between the ages of 18 and 40. Those in the age bracket of 20–21 had already been subject to the Military Training Act of May 1939 which anticipated a declaration of war. Between October 1939 and June 1941 the registration of men proceeded in a series of stages, from those aged 22–23 to those aged 39–40. Those exempted from call up were in a number of 'reserved occupations', such as post office telegraphy and molten steel work. The government's manpower requirements committee recommended a radical revision of these procedures so that women workers could supply the anticipated shortfall in the labour required for the production of munitions. The War Cabinet in January 1941 approved a plan to direct people into work that made goods deemed essential for the war effort. There were to be 'protected establishments' rather than 'reserved occupations'; women between the ages of 20 and 30 were registered (a range later extended to 18–50); the liability of men to call-up was extended to the age of 46.

These provisions were not all fully implemented, but they gave the authorities the discretion they needed to meet any major contingency.

The numbers of people in Ham and Petersham affected by these regulations are difficult to identify precisely. It is also impossible to discover how many men volunteered for military service without waiting for their call-up. But the statistics available suggest that at least 1,800 men would have been liable to conscription or direction of labour. Sadly the only definitive statistics are those giving the number of people who lost their lives.

The national scheme for compulsory military service left ample room for volunteers to man 'civil defence' organisations on 'the home front'. Fears of bombing and of gas attacks led government to construct a system of 'home security' long before the outbreak of war, relying largely on voluntary labour. The Munich crisis of September 1938 and the fall of France in May–June 1940 aroused sufficient concern on both occasions to boost the number of volunteers coming forward, particularly among women.

The two most important women's organisations were the Women's Voluntary Service (WVS) and the Women's Land Army (WLA), both formed as it became apparent that war was imminent. In June 1938 the Home Secretary invited Lady Reading to be the director of a Women's Voluntary Service for Air Raid Precautions; in June 1939 the Minister of Agriculture called upon Lady Denman to head the Women's Land Army. The response to these appeals was generous. The WVS enrolled 32,000 recruits; the WLA had 30,000 'land girls' by the end of 1943. In spite of all her contacts in the National Federation of Women's Institutes which she had chaired, Lady Denman had great difficulty in gaining acceptance of paid female labour on farms. Lady Reading had only a few paid employees; the vast majority of WVS members were unpaid volunteers who turned their hands to doing whatever practical work seemed necessary in an emergency. They fitted well into the array of other services when called upon to distribute food or clothing to the homeless or to help housewives whose homes had been bombed.

The WVS in Richmond was led by Mrs. V. H. Nicol. She was particularly prominent at the meetings held during Women's War Work Week (16-23 July 1941) when Ernest Bevin, then Minister of Labour, made a special visit to the town in order to encourage local women to go into munitions production. There was a meeting in the Ham Institute and an exhibition in the Royalty Kinema.

The apparatus for 'air raid precautions' (ARP) was complicated. It embraced not only a network of air raid wardens but also the fire and ambulance services, and was therefore entrusted to collaboration with the police and to the management of local authorities. The latter were requested by government in 1935 to draw up ARP plans, and by Act of Parliament in 1937 to seek approval of what they proposed. The government secretly in 1938 divided the country into regions, each of which had a special commissioner who was authorised to coordinate civil defence services and to take charge of public order in an emergency. Sir John Anderson as Lord Privy Seal was the minister in charge of all civil defence arrangements, including the distribution of the garden air raid shelters that carried his name. Herbert Morrison took over as the 'Minister of Home Security' in October 1940. Like the heads of the three armed services, he was given his own 'war room' – housed for most of the war in Cornwall House near Waterloo Station. There were pre-war training courses that were designed to prepare all the different categories of staff for bomb damage and gas contamination. These courses created rescue and demolition parties and decontamination squads. The Munich crisis gave the authorities an opportunity to distribute 38 million gas masks, to test siren warnings and to inspect blackout material. The experimental evacuation of children from London exposed weaknesses. Perhaps the most delicate questions arose from the establishment of the Auxiliary Fire Service (AFS). The government wished to increase the labour available to extinguish any conflagrations caused by enemy action but found itself with an awkward mixture of full-time and part-time workers in shifts.

All the different ARP components had to learn how to collaborate at night in the blackout. So much of the pre-war training had been based on the assumption that the Germans would only bomb in daylight. The authorities began to look for what they called 'interchangeability' – the transfer of skills learnt under one branch of the ARP to the demands of the moment in another. Those who had learnt about rescuing people from rubble or stretcher-bearing in the ambulance service might play the same roles with fire-fighters. The number of volunteers involved in ARP work is difficult to quantify. There were, for example, at one stage of the war around 1.4 million firemen and over 250,000 in the personnel of the post-raid services.

Members of the Local Defence Volunteers (LDV) better known as 'the Home Guard' were often called upon to take part in civil defence operations, but they lacked the specific training that had been given to ARP personnel in anticipation of bombing. Although there had been attempts before 1938 to incorporate volunteers into home defence, the government in forming the LDV was in fact improvising in response to public demand rather than defining a clear role for unpaid soldiers within the framework of GHQ Home Forces. There was a great deal of confusion, and scare stories circulated by rumour that German agents were being landed to organise 'a Fifth Column'. It seemed likely that local people in some places would set up their own brigades. Anthony Eden as minister for war decided that it was politic to call for national volunteers; he made a broadcast on 14 May 1940.

The evacuation of the British Expeditionary Force from Dunkirk took place between 27 May and 4 June 1940. By the beginning of August 1.4 million men had volunteered to join the LDV. Winston Churchill began using the term 'the Home Guard' and encouraged others to follow his example. But there continued to be much uncertainty about the status and validity of these volunteers. As far as the Chiefs of Staff were concerned, what mattered in the plans to counter any German invasion were the disposition of regular soldiers and the secretly prepared Auxiliary Units trained to resist a German occupation. The place of the Home Guard within the Army structure of command was not clear until the end of 1941.

A lot depended at the local level on the morale and purpose that might be induced by the presence of veterans from the First World War in each platoon and on the leadership that might be given in those units commanded by officers who were retired regulars. The Richmond Home Guard included around 140 men divided into three platoons, each commanded by a retired regular. They were in the habit of training either in Richmond Park or on Ham Common. The commander of the Ham and Petersham platoon, Lt. Col. A. T. Amoore, set up his headquarters in South Lodge, Ham Common. Known for his dislike of 'bumph' and 'red tape', he subsequently took over command of the whole brigade for which he secured battalion status as the 63rd Surrey (Richmond) Battalion Home Guard. In various exercises and practice fights its chief rival was the 53rd Surrey (Hampton Court & Molesey) Battalion. The worst night of the 'blitz' locally was that of 29 November 1940. Members of the Home Guard were on duty that day for over 14 hours because they had to keep the public away from unexploded bombs. On one occasion in 1942 the Richmond contingent were dressed in Nazi uniforms in order to be the invading force which Hampton Court & Molesey were ordered to stop (see pp 33–4).

Without any expectation of payment for taking the time and the trouble to deal with the emergencies caused by bombing, those who had the opportunities to contribute to civil defence seem to have acquired a strengthened sense of needing to survive in adversity. The morale of the civilian population was difficult to assess. Individuals reacted differently to the restrictions imposed by the shortage of consumer goods and by the arbitrary powers taken by the authorities. The regime of austerity in daily living came in some degree to be associated with the 'Utility Scheme' put forward in 1942 soon after the introduction of clothes rationing. The scheme was intended to standardise products at a level of prices which poorer families could afford. Government officials laid down specifications for goods to which the scheme was extended, such as furniture, and even clothes, so that each item produced could carry the 'utility mark'. The Board of Trade organised a campaign directed at housewives called 'make do and mend'.

The two most obvious restrictions beyond those in affecting the marketing of goods were the censorship of information and the requisitioning of private property. Each of these constraints had been planned in secret before the outbreak of war. From 1935 onwards preparations were made for the creation of a Ministry of Information that would regulate the press and broadcasting, and devise exercises in propaganda for 'the home front'. From 1936 onwards the Office of Works began to prepare a register of property that might be commandeered by the armed forces or by government departments that might be evacuated from London. Local authorities in 1939 were requested to submit the names of houses and owners that might be made immediately available, and the Emergency Powers (Defence) Bill was drafted to give government the powers of requisitioning as soon as they became necessary. When the war came the Office of Works had 200,000 names on its register, because the armed forces had exaggerated their requirements; the number of its regional offices was expanded to meet this demand.

Local newspapers, such as the *Richmond & Twickenham Times* and the *Richmond Herald*, were obliged, like national newspapers, to follow the censorship rules and to accept a rationing of the newsprint available. They were not, for instance, allowed to reproduce photographs of damage that might be fed back to the enemy. They therefore have to be used with care as sources of local history.

INTERLUDE

A portrait of Ham and Petersham in 1939

If you were transported back to this area as it was in Autumn1939, you would find Petersham much the same externally. Opposite the Dysart Arms there was the old Russell School in Richmond Park, and the area around the old Gate Houses would not have modern houses, but would have village shops, including the Post Office and a garage. Sandy Lane was built up on the south side, but the north side was still open land. But Ham would be a much smaller place, with Ashburnham and Woodville Roads terminating at Sheridan and Stretton Roads. The site of the rows of shops in Ashburnham Road and Ham Street were part of Secrett's Farm. A comparison of the map overleaf with that published in *Ham and Petersham at 2000* will show how much housing development was still to come. Several of the large houses fronting on the Common would have much larger grounds attached, where post-war private housing developments have taken place; where Parkleys now stands was part of Ham Farm, one of three still operating in the area. Incidentally, houses around the Common had names, not numbers, and there were two called Rose Cottage, one on the north side and one on the west. The A307 was still a narrow bottleneck that gave concerns to the Civil Defence authorities in case bombs should close it; a private road from Petersham to Sudbrook Lane (now obliterated by new houses at one end, and closed up halfway along) allowed for some emergency access, but would hardly have served heavy traffic. There were five public houses (two now replaced by private housing). The Russell School and the Ham Schools (now St Thomas Aquinas Church) served as Junior schools, but for secondary pupils it was necessary to use the 65 or 73 bus to Richmond. Four churches were there, the ancient church of St Peter's, St Andrew's (known sometimes as Ham Church), the Free Church in Lock Road, and All Saints in Bute Avenue. For Catholic worship and education it was necessary to travel to Richmond. Ham Street and Back Lane were there, the former still much in its present aspect, and the latter running as far as the top of Woodville Road, containing some shops and houses since replaced. On the common was a First World War gun, taken as scrap metal, and cows grazed there. The Pond was not at its best. A searchlight was sited in Park Road (now Ham Gate Avanue.As the Kingston border (half-way along the shops now on the Parade, and marked by a boundary stone) was reached, most,

Ham & Petersham in 1939. (Based on the map by John Plant)

but not all of the present shop premises were there. And there were no traffic lights of any description.

There were no Council facilities locally; private functions could be held at the Village Hall in Bute Avenue, the Institute in New Road (which also functioned as the Hall of St Andrew's Church) and the Lawrence Hall Hotel on the Common (now the Cassel Hospital). Most social organisations were run by the churches. There were two possibilities of having a Parish Hall for St Andrew's. In May 1939 it was hoped that Buckminster Estates would erect a Hall and rent it to the Church, but nothing came of this. Later Kingston suggested building an ARP hall in the Parish, available for general use at times; this also came to nothing.

Ham River Grit Company's lorries loading up. (David Williams' collection)

There was little local employment available: the major local employers were the Leyland works (later Hawker's) on the borders of Kingston borough, and the Ham sand and gravel workings. One small workshop for precision engineering existed. Shop, hotel and domestic work was available, as was a limited amount of farm work.

SHOPS IN HAM AND PETERSHAM

In 1939 the following shops were listed as being open:
Petersham Road:

222 Boot and shoe repairer
305 Dyson, baker
311 Schackell, draper and
    Post Office
327 Gray, beer seller

329 Spratley, tea room
337 Morffew, boot repairer
339 Chinnery, grocer
343 Povey, butcher (later licensed
    as a slaughterhouse)

Ham Common: Adams's Garage & Mason, tobacconist
Back Lane:

2 Jessop, newsagent

4 Kent, fishmonger

Ham Street:

4 Knight, beer seller
11 Fieldson, grocer
12 Dunkley, confectioner
24 Ham valet service

26 Rosser, bootmaker
31 Birch, butcher
33 Kent, greengrocer

Upper Ham Road:

9 Greenwood, dairyman

(Of these, only one remains today – Dunkley, now a grocer at a
different number.)

   In addition there were the following shops, in Ham Parade, then
part of the Borough of Kingston, and all in *Richmond Road*:

297 Ham Common service station

299 W. G. Stanton tobacconist and
    Post Office
301 M. Vallance, greengrocer
303 Dendy's store, grocer
305 Morell & Howells, chemist
307 Tudor Wool Shop
309 Parade Salons
311 Youngton's, ladies' outfitters
313 Circulating library
315 Sidney Horspath, domestic
    stores
Alfred Duck, boot repairer

319b J. H. Ledbetter, radio
    dealer
321 Showroom for service
    station
323 Beales Bros, butchers
418 J. A. Bush, ladies' hair-
    dresser
418a Eileen, dressmaker
420 H. T. Elcombe,
    confectioner
422 F. P. Dagnati, snack bar
424 Keens, grocer
426 W.   J. Finch, green-
    grocer

428 H. F. Gadmark, fishmonger

CHAPTER TWO

The RADAR story

Village life in Petersham was dominated after September 1940 by the presence of a secret establishment devoted to research and training on the use of radar for anti-aircraft guns and searchlights. All Saints' Church, the Vicarage, Petersham Village Hall, and Elm Lodge as well as three other houses were commandeered by the government. For the duration of the war these buildings were occupied by Anti-Aircraft Command, by an extension of the Ministry of Supply, and finally by part of the Army Operational Research Group. The vicar, a bachelor who moved to live in the Old Stables on River Lane, continued to serve the parish from St. Peter's Church.

This establishment was known locally at the time as 'the Radio School', because of the large number of cadets at Elm Lodge who spent a short time in local billets while attending training courses. But it also belonged to an extensive network of civilian scientists promoting the development of radar for both defensive and offensive purposes. Their work was protected by the Official Secrets Act, and their studies covered four locations in which radar sets might improve the accuracy of fire: fighter aeroplanes, anti-aircraft guns, bombing aircraft flying at night, and the combination of aeroplane and ship that sought to destroy enemy submarines. Work on designing appropriate radar apparatus for all four locations was undertaken in Britain largely by the Telecommunications Research Establishment and in the United States by the Radiation Laboratory in the Massachusetts Institute of Technology. Cooperation between British and American experts on radar can be compared to the research teams of the Manhattan Project that led to the creation of the first atomic bomb.

The scientists in the Vicarage and in huts on the Vicarage garden undertook 'operational research' – studying how guns were fired and how radar was used. The Gun Laying Mark I radar sets were fixed to anti-aircraft guns for the first time in Raynes Park on the night of 19/20 September 1940. Other scientists had studied the reactions of pilots in RAF Fighter Command to instructions given from ground radar; those in Petersham were charged with studying the ineffectiveness of anti-aircraft fire. The guns made a great deal of noise that was considered valuable in boosting civilian morale during an air raid, but they rarely hit enemy planes. The first task was to measure the levels of success that could be attributed to the location of the gun batteries or the system that regulated the accuracy of their aim. At the centre of all the Petersham scientific endeavour was 'gun-laying radar'.

The group originally brought together for this work in July 1940 was known affectionately among those with access to radar secrets as 'Blackett's circus'. It began its operations in central London, first at Savoy Hill House and then at Brettenham House near Waterloo Bridge, before being posted to Petersham. Blackett himself described it as 'one of the first groups to be given the facilities for the study of a wide range of operational problems, the freedom to seek out these problems on their own initiative, and sufficiently close contact with the Service operational staffs to enable them to do this' [1].

The whole enterprise was initiated by Professor A.V. Hill, the secretary of the Royal Society, who had been in charge of anti-aircraft gun research during the First World War. He recommended that General Sir Frederick Pile, the officer in charge of the Anti-Aircraft Command, should appoint Professor Patrick Blackett as his scientific adviser, and that he himself should find appropriate candidates for 'the circus'. Hill's standing in radar research, like that of Blackett, rested on being a member of the Air Ministry Committee chaired by Professor Tizard. They had both been closely involved in the secret promotion of radar from 1934 onwards. Hill was also anxious to secure collaboration with the Americans, an idea first officially put forward in May 1939. There were difficulties on both sides. But in March 1940 Hill went to Washington DC, technically as an air attaché in the British Embassy. but in practice as the chief negotiator for some kind of British scientific mission. The creation of 'Blackett's circus' was one of the immediate consequences of the discussions that followed his return.

Hill proposed 'a frank offer to exchange information and experience'; he had the full backing of Lord Lothian, the British ambassador to the United States. Churchill and the War Cabinet agreed in late July 1940 to send a mission via Canada to the United States under the leadership of Tizard. The Americans set up the Radiation Laboratory in response to these exchanges, and its team

---

[1] Blackett: *Studies of War: Nuclear and Conventional* (Oliver & Boyd 1962) p.206

of scientists under Louis Ridenour began immediately to concentrate on the development of 'gun-laying radar' for anti-aircraft guns. Their priority was to see if they could design a system which would allow the radar to track an enemy aeroplane automatically by 'locking on' to the target and give what in British parlance was called 'unseen fire control'. Such a system required stronger and narrower beams.

Patrick Blackett on his arrival in Petersham knew that the most precious secret being shared with the Americans was the invention of the cavity magnetron, which sent high powered radio beams of a 10 centimetre wave length or less. The equipment he was examining in his 'operational research' had been designed and produced long before the prospect of 'the centimetric revolution' that made it possible to create microwaves.

Anti-Aircraft Command assumed that the soldiers manning its gun batteries would have difficulty in making the best use of 'gun-laying radar' which did not 'lock on' to its targets. It decided to train a cadre of officers who could be posted to each battery and improve the radar then available simply by giving them a thorough knowledge of its basic principles. The 'Radio School' set up in Petersham alongside the research scientists was regarded as a 'university of radar' open only to those with first or second class honours degrees. Its first principal, Jack Ratcliffe, epitomised the practice of recruiting eminent scientists capable of keeping abreast of current research and of applying recent findings to the teaching syllabus. He had been the head of the radio ionosphere research group in the Cavendish Laboratory of Cambridge University and was therefore an expert on the reflection of radio waves. At the outbreak of war he had joined the Telecommunications Research Establishment, heading the group using a new type of ground radar equipment. He in fact ran the research side as well as the school for a short time after Patrick Blackett was invited in March 1941 to move from Anti-Aircraft to Coastal Command, which wanted to use his experience in the battle of the Atlantic against German U-boats.

People in Petersham may have been surprised to meet Americans and Canadians attending the Radio School. The great achievements of the Tizard mission in setting up Anglo-American scientific collaboration were the arrangements that brought together civilian scientists and serving military officers in the design and testing of each innovation. The American armed forces sent men to Petersham before the United States entered the war in December 1941, because they wanted their personnel to benefit from direct contact with others already in action. The Canadian Signals Regiment took over Kingston Girls School. For their first visit two Canadian officers were given a map reference and a code phrase 'Thy Kingdom Come'; it took them some time to discover the location because they did not immediately see that the code phrase was carved into a panel over the main door of All Saints' Church. The Canadians were dispersed to man different batteries, some even in the Orkney and Shetland Islands; the Canadian Radio Location Unit formed in January 1942 manned radar stations on the south coast.

The Petersham scientists in both research and training had close contact with the Telecommunications Research Establishment and with the Air Defence Research and Development Establishment supervised by John Cockcroft, another prominent member of the Tizard mission. One of the features of collaboration between scientists and serving officers was attendance by both sides at what were called 'the Sunday soviets', a term coined during the London blitz when Air Marshal Sir Philip Joubert used his house in Bournemouth at the weekends. As the assistant chief of staff responsible for radio and radar in the RAF, he got into the habit of visiting TRE nearby at Worth Matravers on Sundays for informal discussions. The staff in Petersham inaugurated similar seminars. Those living in Petersham grew accustomed to seeing men of high rank going for a drink in *The Fox & Duck* or *The Dysart Arms* after one of these sessions.

The most obvious effects on village life of the presence of so many combinations of civilians and military were the noises and inconveniences of regular movements by staff car, lorry, motorcycle and caravan. Those in charge of 'operational research' equipped lorries as mobile laboratories that could carry cameras and other tools to be used by those observing an anti-aircraft battery in action; they also used caravans. These 'recording vans' designed in Petersham in the autumn of 1941 became important vehicles to assist the observation of battles in Europe after D-Day. Those being trained came in buses from their billets in Richmond or were taken by car to see war rooms and aerodromes; they were also transported regularly to the school's annexe at Saltdene near Brighton. It is difficult to estimate how many cadets were billeted in the village itself. The presence of the Radio School meant that on any given day there would be at least 160 preparing to use the canteen set up in the basement of the Village Institute. The resident population of the parish was around 800.

Local people grew accustomed to seeing regular changes in the number of trainees taking courses at the Radio School, but were of course poorly informed about the character of the authority organising the research. After August 1941 when Jack Ratcliffe moved back into the Telecommunications Research Establishment and handed over to Patrick Johnson the management of the School, then still serving the needs of Anti-Aircraft Command, the research staff came under the supervision of the Air Defence Research and Development Establishment which was part of the Ministry of Supply then responsible for recommending which contracts to place in the manufacture of 'gun-laying radar'.

The research agenda for two years (1941–3) was therefore dominated by designing and testing improvements made possible by the microwaves generated in the cavity magnetron. The Gun Laying Mark II radar set was the first to have 10cm wave length; Mark III the first to have a single cabin for both transmitting and generating radio beams. The Petersham scientists were part of a British team that worked in parallel with American and Canadian counterparts. The basic problem was how to link data from the radar to the predictors which measured the distance, height, and range of any aircraft caught in the radio beam, and then how to link the predictors' instructions to the mechanisms of the guns. There were also methods of applying the same techniques to searchlights.

All Saints' Church and the adjoining Hall provided excellent covers for tests of all kinds. They also gave space for trainees in the School to handle equipment. Both these buildings had been given to the village by Mrs. Warde; their presence probably explains why Petersham was chosen as the site for 'Blackett's circus'. The church could be used for military hardware because it had never been consecrated. The large garden of the Vicarage had been acquired as the plot on which to build a new parish church, a scheme made redundant by Mrs. Warde's gift. The potential of Petersham may have been spotted simply by those who were in the Richmond Park AA batteries. The church and hall were used for experiments with radar cabins, trainers, searchlights and predictors, and for practical instruction; they were large enough to take receivers picking up signals from transmitters on the golf course.

Experiments were also undertaken in the open, using balloons and hiring aircraft. For Petersham the most dramatic event was the occasion in 1943 when an Avro Anson aeroplane crashed onto the roof of Elm Lodge. Fortunately the school principal at that moment was not in his office; he had taken the afternoon off to go to a

Richmond cinema.

The outcome of all this activity was less than its leaders had hoped for. The Gun Laying Mark III set was not put into production until March 1943. A Canadian model was manufactured and distributed in Australia and South Africa. The American team in the Radiation Laboratory successfully designed and tested a set that 'locked on' to its target. This achievement was based on an adjustment in the radio beam which placed it slightly off centre and then on a rotation that formed a cone. A target caught in the overlapping signals from two cones could be tracked automatically. The American Army in April 1942 began manufacturing a radar set called SCR 584 using this method. When Hitler launched his V1 rocket attacks on Britain in 1944, Anti-Aircraft Command managed to acquire these American machines so that they could destroy as many of these weapons in flight as possible over open ground.

From February 1943 onwards the research agenda of the Petersham staff was determined by a 'control group' in the War Office. This shift of responsibility was a direct consequence of the success of 'Blackett's circus' in convincing the Army Council that it should adopt the practice of 'operational research' as a whole in all theatres of war, and not confine its benefits to Anti-Aircraft Command. The Army Council took the initiative after the failure of its coastal batteries to fire on the German battleships, *Scharnhorst* and *Gneisenau*, which had passed unscathed through the Straits of Dover in February 1942. It insisted on taking over from the Air Ministry all the work on problems that arose when its radar sets were jammed. Sir Charles Darwin was appointed War Office scientific adviser. After further discussions the Army Organisational Research Group was set up with headquarters in Ibstock Place, Roehampton. The Petersham establishment became simply section No.1 alongside nine other sections across the Army as a whole. These included sections devoted to coastal gunnery, signals, and infantry.

The requisitioned buildings were restored to their owners in April 1946. The Vicar, the Rev. R. S. Mills (1882–1971), who was the incumbent of St. Peter's from 1929 to 1963, wrote in the March 1946 issue of *The Petersham Leaflet*: 'the establishment of the Radio School here involved many of us in inconveniences and compelled us to reduce our parochial duties to a minimum. It is no longer secret that some of the most important experiments that led to discoveries which made British radar the extremely efficient instrument of war that it came to be, were carried out in Petersham Vicarage'. This praise for local scientists was understandable but a little exaggerated, because it neglected to mention the complicated network of consultations across all the institutions involved, including the American. The contribution of Petersham to the victory of the Allies was as much through operational research as through radar development.

CHAPTER THREE

Camp 020: Latchmere House

At the outbreak of War, Latchmere House, a Victorian building that had been owned by the Army since the First World War, and used firstly as billets and later as a convalescent home for shell-shocked officers, lay unused. It had been extended to accommodate some 30 hospital cells, including padded ones, for those receiving treatment. It lay in a secluded part of Church Road, Ham, flanked by the Common on one side, and with farmland from the main road to St Andrew's Church on the other; beyond the Church were a few large houses: it was thus an ideal site for top secret work with its proximity to London. So, when a decision was made to establish an interrogation centre for enemy spies, much of the necessary accommodation was already in place, needing only equipping with listening devices and the essential security measures. Additional accommodation was provided in new outbuildings and Nissen huts, to accommodate staff. There was only one entrance to the site, which was surrounded by a tall wooden fence, and additional barbed wire around the inner compound. Passes were needed to show to the Military Police on the gate, and there were, in all, four checks for those coming and going. Even the few immediate neighbours were subjected to security clearance (it was not recorded if the Vicar was among them). The name 'Camp 020' was not given until December 1941.

MI5 was expanded from 133 personnel in 1938 to 838, including 634 women, by early 1941. By the end of July 1940 27,000 aliens had been detained nationally, though most of them posed no threat to the War effort. The public were made aware of the dangers posed by spies with a poster campaign using the slogan 'Careless talk costs lives' that featured cartoons of such situations as two women on a bus with Hitler in the seat behind listening to their talk, or a young lady at a party talking indiscreetly to a spy. Films were also made dramatising the risks, and showing how spies might be detected. All this was a far cry from humdrum normal life, but the message had to be got home. At one point an international theatre organist, a frequent performer on the BBC, was not heard for some time, prompting rumours that he had been conveying messages to the enemy by musical methods. He later broadcasted to make the point that rumours were not in the national interest. The local danger was highlighted just before the outbreak of war, when a

Richmond resident was in court, accused of espionage (*see Richmond History 30*).

Germany, on the other hand, was recruiting and landing spies in several parts of the British Isles. It was so confident of a successful invasion that spies' equipment and training were centred around passing information regarding retreating British armies on their own soil. They were not the dedicated and skilful agents familiar from fiction writers, but often somewhat pathetic and careless characters. Of the 21 landing in 1940, all but one were captured: he committed suicide. They came by small boats, aeroplanes, U-boats or parachute. Three became double agents, five were executed and the remainder interned. Thereafter they came in posing as refugees, and in total 33,000 were questioned by MI5. Any proved or suspected agents were quickly sent to Ham. Their full stories can be found in the secret history files of the former Public Record Office, now available as *Camp 020: MI5 and the Nazi Spies*,[1] an official history largely written by Lieutenant-Colonel Stephens that has proved invaluable in providing material for this section of the current book. Thus 'Latchmere' (from Middle English 'lache', meaning a slow, sluggish stream, and 'mere;) assumed a new identity that ensured its place in history. It was said the 'The story of Ham is stranger than fiction, indeed as a work of fiction it would violate the probabilities'.

By 1940 Germany was without sources of information from the UK because of success in rooting out of spies and of interment. It was thought that only two afternoons a week would be enough for the proposed centre to do its work; in fact it was kept busy at all hours for six years. On 10 July that year, Latchmere opened, and on the 27th the first inmates arrived, consisting of British subversives, important enemy aliens and refugees who entered via the Dunkirk evacuation. This group did not merit much attention, consisting of 'treacherous, shabby nonentities' according to the Commandant. The British Fascists were, however, all to well aware of their legal rights at the time when Latchmere was not formalised under Defence Regulations. By October 1940 Ham was ready for its proper function, with spies having no rights under the Geneva Convention. A handicap was that there was no pool of intelligence officers trained in interrogation and the number of 'breakers' throughout the war could be counted on the fingers of one hand. Another handicap was that the Army had very little sympathy for the Intelligence Service; many officers sent there were quite unsuitable until the Camp Commandant was allowed to hand-

[1] Now published by Bloomsbury Academic

pick all the staff. Control was assumed by MI5, not by the Army, despite its ownership of the site. Camp 020 began to concentrate on the more serious cases, and all British suspects were transferred elsewhere. The Royal Victoria Patriotic school in Wandsworth was a screening centre for all aliens arriving from enemy territory. At the head of Camp 020 was Lieutenant-Colonel Robin William George Stephens, a temperamental authoritarian known as 'Tin Eye', probably because of his thick monocle or of the steely gaze that emanated from it. Although a figure of terror to inmates, whom he abhorred with an intensity that verged on the obsessive, he seems to have been much liked by his close colleagues. His fondness for making sweeping statements for pure impact and entertainment value led him into trouble after the war when in charge of Bad Nenndorf camp, where he faced a court-martial for claims of ill-treatment and brutality, both of which were against the principles he laid down at Latchmere from the start. He was acquitted of all charges. He was a formidable linguist, speaking, reading and writing in Urdu, Arabic, Somali, Amharic, French, German and Italian with varying degrees of proficiency. From the start, despite his implacable hatred of the enemy, he ruled that there must be no physical violence involved: the object of interrogation was firstly to elicit as much information regarding the network of spies as possible, and then to endeavour to 'turn' the prisoners to become agents on behalf of Britain.

The first spies arrived in Britain on 3 September 1940, a group of four entering along the Sussex coast at Dungeness and Rye, towed over in fishing boats by a German minesweeper, and transferred to two dinghies for eventual landing. The party consisted of a German and three Dutchmen, carrying their transmitter, some food and personal belongings. One of the Dutchmen went to a local Inn and got into conversation with an Air Raid Warden over drinks. He soon began to make enquiries as to the disposition and number of British troops in the area; on being asked for his identity card, he claimed to be a refugee, saying 'we' arrived last night. He was promptly detained, and his slip of the tongue revealed that there were other suspects in the vicinity. Meanwhile his German companion sent messages demanding that an aeroplane be sent to pick him up; the two remaining Dutchmen took their equipment across the coastal road hoping to find a safe hiding place, but were seen by two British officers in a car, and promptly arrested. The remaining member of the party approached a group nearby asking where he was, and was detained until the Police arrived. All this may sound like an episode from *Dad's Army*, and was indicative of the unprofessional nature of many of the spies who were landed. They arrived at Latchmere on 6 September, the first actual spies to be interrogated there. The full account of their interrogations can be found in *Camp 020* together with the other case histories. Three of the quartet were executed after trials at the Old Bailey and the remaining one detained until the end of the War, then deported. They had all been assured before landing that the German armies would soon invade, and would rescue them.

There was no established manual for Colonel Stephens and his team to use, and no pool of experienced interrogators available for recruitment. Since no interrogations were carried out in English, should the officer responsible not speak the prisoner's language, an interpreter was present. On arrival at Ham the suspect was stripped and body searched, including a dental examination after writing materials were found in a false tooth of one suspect. Prison clothing was issued, with large white diamond-shaped patches on them. The prisoner remained standing throughout, and Stephens' rule was 'No chivalry, no gossip, no cigarettes'. The prisoner was only allowed to speak when spoken to and was expected to answer questions without interruptions or gesticulations. His identity was to be fixed at an early stage. There was to be no violent behaviour on the part of the interrogator; the only incident of this kind from a visiting officer led to a demand by the Home Secretary that Latchmere should revert to civilian control, but the Director General of MI5 gave an assurance that this kind of behaviour would not happen again, so control remained as it was. Pressure was attained by the personality of the questioner, tone, rapidity of questions, insistence on immediate answers and recapitulation. Other psychological methods included the threat of execution (14 out of the wartime total of 16 spies executed came through Latchmere, one of them being considered significant enough to be shot at the Tower of London). No promises or bargains were allowed, and the first interrogation was broken off when a confession was obtained. If the initial examination did not produce results, indirect methods were brought to bear, such as bugging of the individual cells, and the use of a 'stool pigeon' or 'sympathy man' recruited from among other former suspects. Further questions might be set in prisoner's cell, and he could be sent for again whatever the time of night, until such time as the goal of the interrogator was achieved. The process was carried out in two weeks, after which either the suspect became a double agent, or was interned at Ham or elsewhere for the duration of the war. All this laid great strain on the prisoner, but the strain on the interrogator was equal, if not greater. There were only three attempts at escape, and only three attempted suicides, one of which was successful. For those interned on a long-term basis, there were five acres of vegetable-growing space and the rural surroundings to relieve the monotony of imprisonment.

At the first interview a board of officers was appointed. One of them interrogated; this had to be done without interruption from the others, although questions might be invited. In urgent cases two officers took summaries of the proceedings alternately. A quick report was prepared within an hour of completion of interrogation. An interpreter sat next to the interrogator where necessary, and a stenographer was present, relieved every half hour. The final threat would be a spell in Cell 14, which in peacetime was one of the padded ones, conveniently opposite the mortuary. In wartime there was little difference between it and other cells, except that it was cold and a little dark. Those inmates who believed in the supernatural said that certain psychic elements were present. Every quarter of an hour a sentry would come, sometimes with food, and finally to take the inmate to permanent detention elsewhere – or worse; this sanction proved successful on many occasions; despite the melodramatic overtones, a final break could be achieved. If not, there remained little hope of success.

The first goal of Camp 020 was to break the stories of the suspects, obtain as much useful information as possible, and then, if possible, 'turning' the prisoner as a double agent. Those from Ham who were persuaded to join the British 'double-cross system', such as agent Zigzag, were managed by the Twenty Committee (20 in Roman numerals = XX, the 'double cross'), run by John Masterman[1]. Ham was known as one of the two most important sources of information, with over 100,000 Intelligence Cards in its registry. It was visited by personnel from other Services and countries, and after D-day American Army officers were detailed to Ham to study what was going on.

Major successes were secured from the confessions of the clerk of the Portuguese Embassy, which led to the imprisonment of a score of Agents in Portugal, and of the Argentine Plenipotentiary to Hitler and Himmler, which established that far from aiming at the domination of Europe only, Hitler's aims were of world domination A Cuban dancer was questioned and a Royal Navy officer (later hanged for treason) who gave away vital information to the enemy.

[1] See J. C. Masterman: *The Double-Cross System* (Yale U. P., 1972)

There were Bulgarian, Dutch and Egyptian suspects also; some of those questioned had stories that would make any spy novel unbelievable. A Greek master mariner sold information concerning ship convoys to the enemy, though convincing himself that he was a friend to Britain. In 1945 an agent arrested by the French was sent to Ham: he proved to have encyclopaedic knowledge of the Abwehr, the German military intelligence organization (*Abwehr* = defence), which proved useful even at that late stage of the War.

All the clerical work was, of course, done through manual typewriters or handwritten records. Among these were the 'Yellow Peril' records, instituted by Colonel Stephens, a summary of the most important information from the extensive personal record of each agent. These could be several pages long, covering every aspect of the suspect's life and work.

On 29 November 1940 a land mine hit the roof of Camp 020, causing severe damage to the Officers' Mess, living quarters and the offices. There was no telephone, heating, water or light, and all windows were blown out. The Camp carried on despite this, and the officers moved to rooms over the cells, thus giving ample scope for bugging devices. Again in January 1941 a lone aeroplane broke through the clouds over Richmond Park and dropped a stick of four bombs over the site, but did no more than break the regimental cap badge of a sentry in his box. He was unhurt, except mentally, probably feeling that his RSM should not have laid a charge against him for being improperly dressed. Following this incident, a reserve camp was set up in Oxfordshire, but was never put to use except as a detention centre. Perhaps these incidents were the result of random bombings, but it is not impossible that some espionage was responsible. On the other hand, given the importance of the work being done at Camp 020, it is likely that Ham would have been far more heavily bombed had more been known about its existence.

After D-Day, Ham's importance did not diminish. Although interrogation centres were set up nearer the front line, 1944 showed a record number of detainees, as is shown by the table opposite.

Inevitably, where there is secrecy, rumours abound. Two of the folk tales of Camp 020 must be corrected. Rudolf Hess, Hitler's right-hand man, flew solo in 1941 and landed in Scotland. He was not brought to Ham, but was taken to an Army interrogation camp in Hampshire. He was not a spy, so would have little useful information to give Camp 020. After the War, when William Joyce (Lord Haw-haw) was captured, he was treated as a traitor, not as a spy having taken out a British passport before the War; in any case he was a purveyor of propaganda, with no relevant information to give.

Table 1: Intake of prisoners

1940: 107   **1941:** 55   **1942:** 67   **1943:** 65   **1944:** 119   **1945:** 57*

*up to 14 September

Table 2: Nationalities of prisoners

Belgian	68	Italian	12
German	77	Portuguese	9
French	64	Polish	9
Norwegian	35	Danish	8
Dutch	31	South & Central	
British	29*	America	16
Spanish	25	Swiss	5
Icelandic	16	Swedish	5

*mostly before October 1940

CHAPTER FOUR

Defence against bombing and the threat of invasion

The arrangements made for the defence of civilians against aerial bombardment provided Ham and Petersham with a direct experience of coming together under the jurisdiction of Richmond long before war was declared. Central government in 1935 required local authorities to begin civil defence planning and to recruit air raid precautions staff. There was a call for volunteers to become ARP wardens. Preparations to defend the country against invasion came under the General Officer Commanding Home Forces. Arrangements to build up a body of Local Defence Volunteers, then called 'the Home Guard', were sudden and arbitrary after the fall of France to German invaders in May-June 1940. There is no surviving evidence in Richmond of the construction of bunkers for the extremely secret body of men in Auxiliary Units which were charged with sabotage against German forces once they had occupied English territory.

Richmond Council n 1937 set up Air Raid Precautions and Allotments committees; the work of the former, which brought together those concerned with the police, the fire and ambulance services, and the first aid societies, was to take priority over other Council business. In 1938 the Council appointed Brigadier A. T. Shakespear to be its full-time ARP organiser with a salary of £400 a year; and permission was granted for the installation of a searchlight on Ham Common to the north of Ham Gate Avenue – land now mostly wooded but then open enough to graze cows. In the same year there were moves to establish a fire post and decontamination centre at the Golf Club House in Sudbrook Park; this did not take place, and the facilities were set up in the Star and Garter Home instead. The key elements in civil defence operations on the ground were the local control room and the links between wardens' posts. The Richmond control room was at the Central Depot in Lower Mortlake Road.

Shelters and gas masks

High on the agenda were the construction of shelters and the distribution of gas masks. On the question of providing air raid shelters, there was initially no provision for them in Ham; instead a sample trench was to be dug to show householders how they might do the same in their own gardens. Later the metal Anderson shelters were provided to local authorities, and these were supplied free to those who could not afford to buy them; even the cost of digging the large holes to erect them was met in such cases. Ham and Petersham entered the war with insufficient ARP protection.

The first local air raid shelters to be built were on Ham Common, in a tunnel on the site of Bute House in Petersham, and in 1940 beside the Russell School in Petersham. The recruitment of volunteers generally, and particularly air raid wardens, had at first met with little success – a borough-wide problem. By the end of 1937 only 55 wardens had been appointed; another 200 or more were required. Hyman Leon, the deputy mayor, who ran a small chain of shops selling dresses, became the chief warden. Ernest Naylor, a heating engineer, who with his wife was killed by the bomb dropped on 9 September 1940 in Bute Avenue, Petersham, was a part-time warden, probably then stationed at the warden's post in the basement of All Saints' Church before the radar teams arrived. The post was moved in April 1941 to the Golf Course.

Trench shelters were the first provided; later some brick ones were erected, and households had the Anderson shelters in gardens or, later, the Morrison indoor shelters that could double up as a family table. For those that did not qualify for the free Andersons, they could be bought at the following rates: for 4 people: £6.14s; 6 people: £8; 8 people: £9.12s; 10 people: £10.18s. Later the prices were increased by rates from 10s to 17s. Initially only 3 were bought: where there were basements to houses, these were strengthened instead. There was only one size of Morrison shelter.

There was a charge for erection if householders were unable or unwilling to do this themselves, ranging from £1.10s to £3. The Anderson shelters went out of production in 1941 owing to shortage of steel, but as there was no new house building in prospect, local demand had probably been met. Some of the Ham gardens were too small to accommodate a shelter. Initially the Morrison shelters did not prove popular, only 14 applications having been received. They cost £7.12s.6d. if purchased.

A basement public shelter was proposed underneath a group of Petersham cottages called 'Mayleigh', but as the cost would have been £140, this did not happen. Surface community shelters were erected, housing 612 on the Ham No.4 estate, and as late as 1944 adjacent to Ham School, to be used by children only during school hours, but open to the public at other times. A shelter at Trefoil House was closed in 1942 due to lack of use.

After the distribution of gas masks all were instructed to carry them regularly. Pupils from the Russell School would be sent home if they did not bring theirs. Regular inspections were recommended, but the response did not seem to be good. A correspondent to a local paper complained that inspectors should not be expected to visit homes for this (Marjorie Lansdale recorded a result of such a visit), but that owners should take them to local posts. In 1944 the Council recorded that only 50% were brought. Ham had no cleansing station in the event of a gas attack; it was suggested that they should share Kingston's; the response was 'having regard to the nature of the area it is unlikely that large congregations of persons would be in the streets, and that most of the houses are provided with baths'.

Air Raid Wardens

In 1939 a large-scale exercise was held for Air Raid Wardens, and the number in training was good, with their meetings well attended. But by the end of the year eight of the Ham wardens were called-up, leaving the responsibilities with the remaining women members and older or exempt men. Their Ham post X was in Ham School, and Y in a hut on the golf course, while the Petersham post was on land opposite the *Fox & Duck*. In 1940, however, the Mayor (who was also Chief Warden) wrote to Y post telling them they were in danger of closure because of lack of volunteers. Joint exercises with the Fire Guards were mounted in 1940, also a display the following year between the *Fox & Duck* and *Dysart Arms*. A special trench for the Wardens was dug in 1940. In 1941 protests were made over the requirements to surrender clothing coupons for their uniforms. But by 1943 enthusiasm seemed to have waned, because there was no response to an appeal for extra volunteers. Daylight ARP duties ended in 1944.

The Fire Guards were of particular importance in dealing with the effects of incendiary bombs, a quantity of which affected Ham in particular. A training lecture was given for them at Trefoil House, and they had social gatherings from 1943, with games and competitions. At this point the stirrup pump should be mentioned, largely for domestic use, though St Andrew's bought two. A recent TV show on antiques showed how they have been forgotten, when an auctioneer had no idea whatsoever of the name or use of this piece of equipment on offer. The pump was vertical, placed in a bucket or other water container, with a support that held the device steady by placing a foot on it. To keep it pumping steadily, the water would need continuous renewing, but it must have doused many a small blaze. An effective counter for incendiaries was a supply of sand to douse the flames.

The *Stretcher Party* was set up in 1940 at the Golf Club. The following year it staged what were called 'interesting' incidents, with the help of the Sea Scouts, who acted as 'casualties' in the *Fox & Duck* shelter, 'Sunnydene' and a garden in Lauderdale Drive. There was a strong social side to this group, who raised money for charity and held a party for 118 children; 50 children were taken to see Cinderella at the Kingston Empire. When the depot was closed in 1942 and absorbed into the rescue services, local social life must have been much duller.

In 1939 the nearest first-aid post at the Star and Garter Home was considered to be too far from Ham, so mobile units were set up in 1940 consisting of doctor, trained nurse and other First Aid personnel following questions at a Labour Party meeting.

It was suggested in February 1941 that the gas cleansing station for Ham should be joint with Kingston, who rejected it saying 'having regard to the nature of the area it is unlikely that large congregations of persons would be in the streets, and that most of the houses are provided with baths.' A special trench was provided for Air Raid Wardens.

The Home Guard

The Richmond Home Guard included around 140 men divided into three platoons, each commanded by a retired regular. They were in the habit of training either in Richmond Park or on Ham Common. The commander of the Ham and Petersham platoon, Lt. Col. A. T. Amoore, set up his headquarters in South Lodge, Ham Common. Known for his dislike of 'bumph' and 'red tape', he subsequently took over command of the whole brigade for which he secured battalion status as the 63rd Surrey (Richmond) Battalion Home Guard. In various exercises and practice fights its chief rival was the 53rd Surrey (Hampton Court & Molesey) Battalion. The worst night of the 'blitz' for Richmond was that of 29 November 1940. Members of the Home Guard were on duty that day for over 14 hours because they had to keep the public away from unexploded bombs. A lot depended at the local level on the morale and purpose that might be induced by the presence of veterans from the First World War in each platoon and on the leadership that might be given in those units commanded by officers who were retired regulars.

A Home Guard sports gala was held in 1941 on Ham Common in aid of the ARP Benevolent Fund, and in the same year the 'A' company was inspected on Ham Common, followed by training exercises. In 1942 boys of 16 became eligible for Home Guard duties; there was no compulsion, but written consent had to be given. Their duties would be with anti-aircraft batteries, and doing plotting previously done by ATS girls. Preference was given to Army Cadet forces, Junior Training Corps, Sea Cadets and Air Training Corps; they wore their present uniform with Home Guard armbands. The Home Guard was stood down in 1944, by which time there was no fear of invasion.

The invasion exercise

In 1942 a German invasion still seemed possible. Councillor Westlake was made district invasion officer. On 12 September 1942 a public meeting at Trefoil House was told that 'arrangements are made for the invasion exercise to take place in Ham and Petersham tomorrow morning. Earliest "Incidents" will have the effect of blocking all road-accesses to the area from Richmond or from Kingston. Shortly afterwards the "enemy" will drop paratroops into Richmond Park, whence they will advance through Ham towards the river with the assumed object of destroying Teddington Lock. To assist the illusion, "enemy" troops will appear in German uniforms and street fighting will develop in Lock Road towards noon.

'In the meantime the whole of the local invasion defence organisation for Ham and Petersham will be mobilised to lend assistance to the Home Guard. Food supplies will be controlled; labour will be requisitioned; would-be refugees controlled and redirected; emergency cooking and sanitation will be demonstrated; and emergency water supplies delivered to the public.

'News will be received by radio and posted upon bulletin boards. So far as casualties are concerned, it is not anticipated that numbers of the rescue services will be able to enter the area; wardens and housewives will therefore assume full responsibility for civilian casualties, supplementing the stretcher squads of the Home Guard. Teams of housewives will be seen at different points removing injured persons with the Richmond housewives' "stretcher party", aid houses will be in operation; and several of the new bicycle trailers will be seen in action for the first time in this district.

'The whole exercise will be covered by running commentaries delivered at suitable points, and the various features have been so timed that the public will be able to follow one of the loudspeaker cars and so to keep track of the whole proceedings.

'An invasion exercise has aptly been described as "an exercise of the people, by the people, for the people", and it is hoped that the people of Ham and Petersham will turn out in force to learn what might be their role under invasion conditions.'

The following week, *Richmond and Twickenham Times* reported: 'As reported more fully in the *"Thames Valley Times"* members of the Home Guard, NFS [National Fire Service], police, ARP [Air Raid Precautions] services, WVS [Women's Voluntary Service] took part in large-scale invasion exercise in Ham and Petersham on Sunday morning.

'How to deal with fires, gas and unexploded bombs, and what to do if gas, electricity and sewers failed were all demonstrated in the course of an imaginary invasion, when Ham and Petersham were assumed to have become isolated. As a concluding item, "invading troops" penetrated as far as Ham and occupied houses in Lock Road and New Road; Home Guards, although delayed by a "panic" amongst residents in Lock Road, quickly rounded up the "invaders" and having taken them prisoner, marched them off for inter-rogation.

'The Mayor . . . the Deputy Mayor . . ., Alderman Mabel Lawrie, Councillor J. W. Westlake, district invasion officer, and the town clerk . . . were present.'

On 17 October eighty members of the South District Women's Institute met at Trefoil House to discuss invasion defence from the women's point of view and suggested that a demonstration should be staged to test the machinery of the Invasion Defence scheme.

PROFILE

Vernon Ward ARA

Vernon Ward (1905–1985) spent most of his life in Hampstead, his birthplace, except for a period when he shared a studio with Noël Syers in Twickenham, *c*1940–1971. He studied at the Slade School immediately after the First World War, but in the inter-war years earned his living as a commercial artist (including work for the magazine *Everybody's*), and as a book illustrator. Later he became famous for his exquisite flower paintings and his many studies of ducks and swans, many of them painted from around Richmond Bridge.

He was declared unfit for military service (Grade C) and became active in Civil Defence, where he was in charge of the maintenance of ambulances in Richmond's ARP depot, according to Syers, who reported that at one stage Vernon Ward was stationed at Montrose House. There he painted several garden studies and a large painting in black-and-white of searchlights picking up German bombers over the nearby Golf Club. Two of his colleagues have left accounts of his wartime service: Laura Dance and Becky Groombridge (who later won a gold medal for Ice Dancing). They do not quite agree:

'We were both given jobs in the local ARP . . . I'm not sure what Vernon was, but we were stationed with stretcher bearers and heavy rescue teams made up mainly of local tradesmen, fishmongers, dustmen and so on, but with no air raids in the early stages of the War, we had rather a lot of time on our hands . . . Later that year [1940] we were moved *en masse* to the Richmond Golf Club (much to the annoyance of the genuine members), a lovely Georgian building surrounded by golf links and trees . . . The thing I remember most was the fun we had chasing each other to work on our bicycles, called, for some reason or other, Strawberry and Blackberry, dodging the cars and buses and eventually arriving at our destination . . . We spent our days pretending to clean ambulances, swotting up our first aid and waiting for the air raid sirens . . . In theory we were all engaged for some purpose on the same level, but social prejudice dies hard . . . (*Laura Dance*)

. . . I was transferred from my Civil Defence post in Sudbrook Park, not the depot she mentions, but in the same park, to an ambulance depot in Friars Stile Road, Richmond . . . I started working on the camouflage nets which were put up for us to work on in our spare time . . . I shall never forget the day that he went,

Vernon Ward's sketches for the Grey Court Nursery murals

aged about thirty-six, for his call-up interview. He phoned me afterwards with a whoop of glee to say that he was C4 and was to be left in Civil Defence. (*Becky Groombridge*)

Vernon Ward played a full artistic part in his time with the Petersham stretcher party. At a social he decorated the recreation hall with a mural showing a stage setting of the *Fox & Duck* with ARP members cartooned in colour in early 19th century costumes. For their dance in aid of the Free French in 1941 his paintings *Marianne* and *Britain's mastery of the sea* were on show in Sudbrook House. Members appeared in another of his paintings *Loading casualties.*

Becky Groombridge wrote: 'I am proud to say now that I helped him with all his wartime posters and his frieze designs for the Ham Common Day Nursery' [she meant, of course the Nursery at Grey Court]. I don't mean on the art side, that was totally his scene'. His *Marianne* was exhibited by *Les Français de Grand Bretagne* in their room overlooking Trafalgar Square, and was used in their 1941 Christmas card.

Information taken from Josephine Walpole, *Vernon Ward: Child of the Edwardian Era* (Antique Collectors' Club, 1988).

CHAPTER FIVE

Dealing with the emergency

The accommodation available in the two villages determined in large measure the contributions they could make to the immediate emergencies of war. Ham had more involvement with the evacuees sent from East London because South Lodge could be converted into a hostel; Petersham played a larger part in making space in its large houses available for public occasions or society meetings because it contained far more buildings that were suitable for such a use. The loss of Petersham Village Hall to Anti-Aircraft Command reduced the number of social activities in the parish.

The Evacuees.

The decision of Surrey County Council was that Richmond was a 'neutral' area, not in need of evacuation; they claimed that there were far too many local authorities asking for such action. Richmond Council appealed against this ruling in 1939 and 1940, though without success. So Ham and Petersham remained full of children, except for those who had private arrangements for living away. There were, however, evacuees in Ham, part of the 1,000 homeless East-enders, mainly from Stepney, that Richmond had agreed to house. They arrived on 13 September 1940, and taken to Ham School playground, shelter and three schoolrooms. By eight o'clock that day, all had been found billets. A centre was set up in South Lodge, consisting of a common room/children's room/reading and rest room containing a piano and with an outside washhouse and an office for the warden; there were to be sewing and cookery classes. A welcome party was held at Ham Institute over the 1940 Christmas holiday, and the Centre was opened by the Mayor in February 1941 with entertainment by the Police concert party. Local people made homeless by air raids were to use the Centre too. The children had their own garden, and the *New Inn* provided allotments. The first anniversary was celebrated with a party and a cake, cut by the Mayor; 80 were present at this. Fortnightly Sunday afternoon social events were laid on with films, including Charlie Chaplin, Popeye, Mickey Mouse, detective and comedy films; gramophone record recitals were also given. A romantic episode came when two of the Stepney evacuees became engaged: they had not met before coming to Ham.

Not all was sweetness and light, however. The WVS ran a clothing depot at Ham, but trouble was caused by women who claimed this was a right, not a privilege. So unpleasant were things that the depot was closed down after only one day, and transferred to Kingston.

An evacuee from Woodville Road was caught shoplifting, pleaded guilty and placed on probation for two years. A lady from West Cottage suggested that other people might offer evacuees their homes rather than hers. She claimed that South Lodge was already turned into a slum by evacuees' laundry and the British Restaurant, and said that the Home Guard were always clearing up after evacuees, who were kept by the State in complete idleness. At the 1941 AGM of the Ratepayers' Association there were complaints that some paid only half the rent of established tenants, but it was explained by Councillor Allum that the Ministry of Health provided subsidies to ensure that rehoused tenants paid the same rate that they paid in Richmond.

When, in 1944, attacks by the V1 flying bombs began, Surrey at last agreed that Richmond should be evacuated. Those who experienced this will remember that they boarded trains without any knowledge of their ultimate destination, but there is evidence that Wigan was the destination of some, if not all, of our local evacuees. A mother from Woodville Road was sent there with 11 of her 14 children, age ranges from 3 months to 14 years; the three eldest remained in Ham in the pair of council houses that had been converted into one to accommodate them when they became part of the local influx following pre-war overcrowding legislation. Wigan had some difficulty in finding a 6-bedroomed house for them, but once settled they were visited by the father, a die caster at the local Leyland factory; he found Wigan quite attractive, and would consider settling there. Another family was less fortunate: their daughter fell from one of the special trains and was killed.

3,657 were evacuated from Richmond; an allowance of one shilling each was given to each child of school age and under as an 'evacuation grant'.

The British Restaurant

A Community Kitchen was established in the East Bungalow of South Lodge (Ham Common) after the house had been requisitioned for accommodating evacuees. The room used formerly housed the South Area Richmond War Refugees committee. The Ministry of Food wanted the cooking to be done with solid fuel. In the restaurant was an open fireplace and individual tables that gave a 'homely' look to the place. The prices set initially were as follows:

Soup and bread 2*d* ; Main course 7*d* ; Pudding 2*d* ; Cup of tea 1d.

For those under the age of 13, main course/pudding was 7*d.*

The main room was reserved for the use of the evacuees. As the accommodation was rather limited, many customers brought their own containers, thus turning the enterprise into an early takeaway: this was the main object. For those who wanted to eat on the premises, a small room was available. As more space was needed, the Council tried to rent two garages on the site, but as the asking price was too high, they were compulsorily requisitioned.

By 1942 the name 'British Restaurant' had been adopted. By January 1944 11,476 meals had been served; in 1945 the typical fare (presumably daily) was 156 bread at 1d, 340 soup at 2d, 753 main course at 9d, 753 puddings at 3d, 530 cups of tea at ½d, totalling £44-15s-5d. Eventually the number of voluntary helpers began to drop off; appeals for extra help were made, but in the end paid staff were brought in. The price of the main course was increased to 11p.

Not all local people were happy with the enterprise. At an AGM of the Ratepayers' Association a member claimed that people from Kingston factories were flocking to Ham for cheap meals, causing cafés to close. A café owner claimed that while Civic restaurants were being allowed unlimited meat, his allowance had been cut down. A correspondent to the local Press from Queen's Road, on the other hand, said it was used mainly by working people and schoolchildren, but few women, and that it had come to stay. A lady from Kew wrote to support her.

Plans were made locally, early in the War, for emergency meal supply in case of extensive bomb damage. Ham School claimed it could supply 1000 3-course meals daily, and the Community Kitchen would be able to step up its output. Not to be outdone, the Women's Institute claimed it could supply a 3-course meal including fish, poultry or meat plus 2-veg at 1s 3p, 1s for 2 courses, less if meat unobtainable.

Hospitality from the large houses

Many wartime functions were held in some of the larger local houses, particularly in Petersham. **Trefoil House** in Petersham was used throughout the war by the local Women's Institute, except for a short time after the bombing of the Russell School. It also housed AGMs of the Ratepayers' Association, and was used for lectures, including the 'invasion' lecture in 1942 and one for the Fire Guards. In **Douglas House** (now part of the German School) a fête for the Richmond Conservative Women was held here in 1942. The swimming pool was opened to the Sea Scouts for their 1942 annual swimming gala, and in 1943 both the gala and their summer show were held here. In 1944 a Garden Fête in aid of 'Salute the Soldier' week was held, with an address by Quintin Hogg, the MP for Oxford who had been invalided out of service overseas with the Rifle Brigade, admission 6*d*. In **Montrose House**, owned at the time by the Carr family of biscuit fame, fund-raising Open Days were held in aid of the District Nurses' funds (admission one shilling) in 1943 and 1944, and the garden was also opened in 1944 for a fete in aid of Prisoners of War arranged by the Richmond Conservative Association. In the **Manor House** a fête in aid of St Peter's parochial funds was held in 1942, and the garden was host to the Richmond divisional Girl Guides' camp. In **Petersham House** (home of Mrs Lionel Warde) in 1944 an Open Day was held in aid of District Nurses' funds, and in the 1940s the annual Garden Party and Gift Day of St Andrew's was held here (though the house was in the parish of St Peter's, nearby). Mrs Warde twice a month put her house at the disposal of one of the many knitting parties held locally, and over 100 garments were sent from them to the troops. In 1942, one or two allotment spaces in the grounds were offered for use. The grounds were opened in 1941 in aid of the YWCA (Young Women's Christian Association). However **Petersham Lodge**, leased to the Council Home for Governesses, was closed, and the Council lease surrendered so that it could be sold privately.

Ham did not possess as many houses that could offer hospitality. At **Langham House** (on Ham Common) the St Andrew's Mothers Union and Women's Fellowship were entertained in the grounds in both 1941 and 1942. At **Ormerley Lodge** the garden fete of St Andrew's was held in 1941 and raised £275. **SudbrookHouse**: Housed the Stretcher Party in the early years of the War (see p.31–).

Fund raising

A principal motive for making large houses available to use for public occasions was fund raising for the many good causes which arose from the war emergencies. These methods of raising money can be listed:

Church schools and Overseas Missionary Societies at the Ham Institute.

District Nursing Association: Two Open Days at Montrose House and one at Petersham House

Free French: Stretcher Party socials & dances raised over £80 by 1941

John Groom's Crippilage: Whist Drive raised over £5

Greater London Fund for the Blind: 12 Sea Scouts collected £15 at Kingston Empire

Merchant Navy Week: The Women's Institute knitting party opened their shop in the Parade to raise money for this.

Merchant Navy Week: The Women's Institute knitting party opened their shop in the Parade to raise money for this.

Merchant Navy Comforts Service: £2 raised by WI.

Merchant Seamen's Fund: Scout craft display raised £2

National Savings: by 1943, Women's Institute had invested over £129. In the same period, the Russell School collected nearly £40. By the end of 1942 the Sudbrook Ward savings group had raised £3993, and the number of savings groups was in double figures, augmented by the jumble shop in the Parade that made £60 in just two weeks in 1940.

Prisoners of War fund: garden fete at Montrose House. Mead Road street party raised £5 in 1940

Red Cross: Dance at Institute raised £8. WI raised £30 via a knitting party

Richmond's warship: target £20,000.

Russian Red Cross: Dance at Lawrence Hall Hotel, but only made £2.10s profit.

Salute the Soldier week (1944).

Soviet X-ray fund: Dance at Institute with 100 people plus Mayor and Mayoress, raised £7.

Wings for Victory (June, 1942): 2 Whist Drives held at Lawrence Hall Hotel; talk at the Ham Institute on Fleet Air Arm with film – admission was by buying Savings stamps; Gala and fete held on Common, including cricket match in comic costumes, auction sale, children's races, treasure hunt, darts, baby show, tug-of-war in which the *Crooked Billet* pub beat the *Ham Brewery Tap* on their way to the final that was won by the Military Police. (Financial result was not good owing to lack of helpers.)

Women's Land Army Benevolent Fund: Lady Cowley organised sale of garden produce, 2nd-hand clothes, fancy goods, gramophone records, books, at the Ham Institute.

Regular contributions to National Savings were made by the Russell School, raising nearly £40 in 6 months.

Special mention should be made of Master John Kempthorne, who raised £2.6s.8d for Merchant Navy Week, hoping to add £10 to the total of £25 he had raised for the War effort in 3 years, including *Aid to Russian Horses*. This included the proceeds from using his toy theatre to show Little Red Riding Hood in his house.

Grey Court nursery school.

Another important local response to the deprivations of war was provision for taking care of the young while those of adult age were either on military service or in weapons production. Both nursery schools and youth clubs were needed.

With many fathers away on national service, and mothers out at work it became necessary for some provision to be made for children of pre-school age. On the face of it there was no suitable building available to house such a project, but a proposal in 1941 was made for a specially designed hut to be erected on a bomb site in Lock Road. The Town Clerk said that there were no suitable houses in Ham, but Alderman Starr protested, saying it was a national disgrace while the War Office could requisition houses for their own use. By February 1942 it was found that the Ministry of Health might have Grey Court available to cater for 50 children, though this by no means solved the problem since 46 mothers with 56 children were engaged on War work. The house was in a dreadful condition, and would cost an estimated £1508 to put right, but the scheme went ahead, and advertisements placed for a Matron, Deputy Matron, 2 assistant nurses, 3 probationer nurses, a cook, a cleaner and a teacher. Another probationer would be appointed if enough voluntary help was not forthcoming. All but three of the staff would be housed in the building. The lowest estimate for conversion was £1,780, and the annual running cost was likely to be £1,673. Part of the lawn was to be used as a playground, and some of the kitchen garden given over to producing vegetables for the project. It was 8 February 1943 before the nursery was ready for use, but when the wife of the Minister of Health performed the official opening ceremony, she declared that it was one of the best Nurseries she had seen. It was equipped with living quarters for staff, 3 large nursery rooms, washroom, dining room and an office for the Matron. Safety gates were installed at the top and bottom of the stairs, and a gas-proof Air Raid Shelter built. The interior walls were decorated in primrose yellow and apple green; a 'local artist' (Vernon Ward, see pp .35-7) decorated two of the rooms with friezes showing Noah's Ark and fairytale scenes. A monthly medical examination was instituted.

The cost per child per day was one shilling, and clothing coupons were needed (some from parents, some from the Board of Trade) to provide overalls, towels, bibs and nappies. In the end, up to 36 children could be accommodated, including (so the Ministry of Health decreed) children of expectant mothers and hospital cases, though not at the expense of working mothers. The initial intake was only 12, and although that figure increased over the weeks, it was always necessary to bring children in from the overcrowded Parkshot nursery in Richmond to make up the numbers. When the flying bombs and evacuation arrived, local registrations dropped to 10, the Council considered closure at that point. At the end of 1944 it was still open, and the Junior section of the Richmond Girls' Training Corps contributed regularly from their toy-making section.

The Boys' and Girls' Clubs

It was decided early in the War that the formation of a club for boys would be a way of keeping them out of mischief; the police were very keen on this. A site was found on which the boys themselves could erect a suitable building. A building was located in Hampton Wick for £100; in addition an air raid shelter was to be built. The Club was to be affiliated to the Sea Scouts and the Air Training Corps. The Ministry of Health was less happy and urged those concerned to defer because of the restrictions on capital expenditure; Richmond asked them to reconsider. In June 1941 the MOH finally approved a site (it appears to have been in Back Lane, though originally proposed for Woodville Road), and by August 1941, St Andrew's church magazine reported, the foundations had been laid Meanwhile the Institute played host to the Club for one night a week, and 40 boys attended, playing a football match against a Twickenham side that same afternoon. The Mayor appealed for help for the Club, calling it 'one of the finest examples of social work in the Borough'. Surrey County Council made a donation for equipment, but funds were still needed for furnishing and more sports equipment. By October the new building was nearing completion, and plans were made for boxing, PT, and football (the team had already played four matches, of which they won one and drew one); the Club had 70 members plus an Army Cadet Corps of 40. The average attendance however was only 20 at first, but doubled later.

At the first AGM, tributes were paid to Police Inspector Edden, whose efforts ensured that the Club carried on in difficult times. At the second AGM it was agreed that the Club should be open to Petersham boys (an indication that Ham still considered itself to be quite separate from its neighbour). There was a problem of getting enough supervisors, but they boys were keen enough to redecorate their clubhouse in 1942; they all had full sports kit, and were happy to consider forming a joint committee with the Girls' Club. Tragedy hit them in 1943 when the Secretary of the Club (who organised the Wings for Victory fête) died at only 44; their Army Cadet Corps formed a Guard of Honour at his funeral. By 1944 they were confident enough to entertain boys from Kingston to billiards, darts and table tennis, no doubt to the accompaniment of the radiogram that the Club owned. The snacks from the canteen on that occasion were said to be 'the best in the Borough'.

In 1942 a proposal was put forward for forming a Girls' Club, though it was thought that accommodation would be a problem. 25 girls joined, hoping for fortnightly dances; they found that the aims were 'Christian citizenship, handicrafts, dramatics, music, talks, ballroom dancing, cycle rides, and hikes'. The subscription was 6d per week, and the Club was to meet three times a week. Eventually three rooms were allocated in South Lodge; a correspondent to the local Press assumed that the Club would spoil the peaceful seclusion of Ham Common . . . with a jazz band every night(!). The acting secretary responded saying the letter 'displays an ignorance of the aims and activities. Not all people were so disposed; . . . support from permanent residents makes it clear that such a venture can be as useful as it is needful.' And so at the end of May the first meeting took place, with handicrafts and a social hour. The next month the first monthly dance was held at the Lawrence Hall Hotel, and a month later games and sports were organised with the Boys' Club. By August the membership was 60, and a drama group was formed with the aim of producing their own version of *Gone with the Wind*. At the first AGM in November, the membership had risen to 80, and the Mayoress became President for the next year. The pressure on accommodation at South Lodge had increased with the growth of the British Restaurant, but the Club's interests were well to the fore. In 1943 Richmond Labour youth committee invited the girls to perform a sketch called *Old Moore's Almanac*; they celebrated their first anniversary in 1943 with another dance at the Lawrence Hall Hotel.

Allotments

Growing plants on allotments were an important part of wartime life, encouraged by the 'Dig for Victory' campaign, because there were great advantages in having home-grown food. The Ministry of Food tried to encourage use of potatoes instead of bread wherever possible, to cut down imports of wheat. A sidelight on imports was the prize of onions offered at a dance at the Lawrence Hall Hotel; clearly a very desirable thing at the time.

Buckminster Holdings offered 4½ acres, housing 67 plots, for rent, early in the War: all but six were taken up initially. Requisitions (particularly undeveloped sites in Lauderdale Drive) and use of 2.74 acres of Green Belt land to the north of Lock Road provided other space. Another acre of Green Belt land was released later, followed by a further two.

There was a certain amount of control over allotment holders. In 1941 the Propaganda Committee wrote to all holders urging them to recruit other holders. An appeal was made to restrict flower growing to only 10% of the plot. There was to be a fine of up to £50 for pilfering. Prizes were given to allotment holders, but in 1944 these were abandoned due to work involved in organizing and judging. That same year a drought brought a ban on watering, but water charges were halved to compensate. Trespassing on allotments, from that year, was made an offence, without proof of damaging being necessary. Growing of fruit was forbidden, which may seem strange, but if bushes or trees were planted it was not possible to secure a rotation of crops. This restriction sometimes caused embarrassment to allotment holders, since when they went to buy fruit, they could be refused, because they did not buy vegetables. At the end of the War Richmond needed 66 acres of allotment land for housing; Buckminster refused to provide an alternative site, so 74 acres at Grey Court was provided instead.

Ham Lands, Petersham Meadows and the River

All the extra work of the war effort heightened the sense of a need for recreation. The land by the river had been for a long time been a playground for Londoners as well as locals.

Access to the river was less free than it is now because of the gravel workings, and the lake in what is now the Thames Young Mariners was of far greater extent, stretching as far as Perryfield Way. But the towpath was free for walking, and at the time of Dunkirk one in six of the 'little ships' could be seen being fitted in Tough's boatyard on the other side of the river. The area from the edge of Buccleugh Gardens to the edge of the gravel workings was much used for recreation during the War, attracting many from outside the Borough by means of its river access and refreshment facilities. Litter, particularly broken glass from bottles, was a problem: in 1942 over 150 paddlers were injured by this and at Whitsun 1944 109 were treated. A girl fell into the river at River Lane in 1942; her rescuer became exhausted and both had to be helped by a second man (both men came from the East End). Drenched, they all repaired to the *Fox & Duck*, where the wife of the landlord agreed to dry their clothes. When she knew one had to get back to work that day, she lent some of her husband's clothes to him; they were returned with a letter of thanks. On the August Bank Holiday a man was drowned, and in 1943 a fisherman also, off Petersham Meadows.

On the Riverside Lands, chairs were being hired out. Proposals for a caravan and camping site for summer entertainment were rejected in 1942. A lengthy Council debate raised questions of sanitation and water supply arrangements. In Autumn 1943 a portable refreshment stall with a 400 gallon container for water was erected east of a timber dump (that had a nominal rent of only 1*s*) near Ham House. The following year new tenders for this were invited: none were received, but Leonard Lee, with his 100-gallon water tank, took over. The income from hire of chairs that year was £255 against £359 the previous one. By 1944 a correspondent complained about camping and fire lighting on the Lands, opposite Eel Pie Island, and Councillor Thompson criticised the behaviour of cyclists who would not keep to the paths provided for them. In 1945 Leonard Lee de Ville continued catering. There was no provision for toilets.

The farm at Petersham suffered an outbreak of foot and mouth disease that started with pigs in 1940; 176 cows had to be destroyed. Because of this Kingston cattle market was closed, but fortunately the outbreak was over within a month. A valuable Jersey cow was fatally injured by broken glass in 1942. The dairymen Hornby and Clark asked for use of part of the Meadows for a refreshment room until the end of the War; the changing room next to the nearby toilets would be used as a tea room. A Mr Dunham of Clapham provided this. Petersham Meadows was under threat in 1945 from Council proposals to site a swimming pool and sunbathing area there.

Heat and cold brought their problems. A drought in 1944 brought restrictions on house use, allotments, car washing and fountains. In contrast early in 1945 it was recorded that people were actually were able to skate from Richmond to Ham on the frozen Thames.

Crimes and misdemeanours

The worst crimes were committed by those who came from outside the Ward. In 1941 two Chiswick brothers were sent to prison for 3 years for robbing Ham Post Office. Just before the end of the War a Sunbury man was charged with theft from a house in Sudbrook Gardens; he took a fox fur coat, a pony skin coat and audio equipment, total value £159.

There was no serious crime reported during the War, but several parts of the community were involved in annoying incidents. Damage to air-raid shelters was caused by youngsters, who also indulged in petty pilfering locally. Fires on the Common seemed to be a regular occurrence; in 1945 6 people were prosecuted for damaging trees and shrubs on the Common.

Having stolen from vending machines, four boys climbed over the fence into the Golf Club and ate the contents; their Probation Officer claimed this was because there was not enough for them to do in the evenings. (This was before the opening of the Boys' Club.) Shoplifting from Bentalls was a popular pastime; a 'perfect wife' was charged with stealing in one visit a bag, a remnant of ribbon (!), a saucepan, a broom head, a tray and a bottle of perfume, total value £2.12s.4d. There was the inevitable crop of fines for speeding (but not down Star and Garter Hill, which was still unrestricted); offertory boxes were taken from St Andrew's Church, also their curtains; an ARP man was fined for being late; prosecutions were made for breaches of the blackout regulations, including the Lawrence Hall Hotel, Martin's Bank, the Ham River Grit Co., and one for Farmer Secrett at Manor Farm, where he claimed that his bull had managed to switch on the electricity at night; a local grocer was fined for refusing to billet a soldier; a dog without a licence incurred a fine for the owner; cyclists were fined for going the wrong way down a one-way street and for jumping a red light; three rabbits were stolen from a neighbour's garden; parents were prosecuted for failing to send their children to school. It seems that nobody was sent to prison for these offences. A more serious case was that of a woman who pulled out some hair from a teenage girl, causing bleeding – the hair was produced in court as evidence. At least nobody was fined for queue-jumping, though this happened to a lady on the other side of the river.

Some harmless fun led to a fine of £1 on each of two charges of assault in 1942. A 10-year-old boy, walking in the snow with his mother threw a snowball at another boy, who then hit the son. The mother claimed she was playing snowballing with four other children when the accused intervened; she told him he was a bully to hit her son, and threw a snowball at him, whereupon he hit her heavily in the face.

An ex-serviceman wrote to the *Richmond and Twickenham Times* in 1944 complaining eloquently about the litter, vandalism, noise from older boys after dark, loud radios, blackout faults, saying 'I see no reason why this part of Ham (Neville Road) should become a race apart, a place that the roads to the City pass by and the rest of the Borough forgets.'

CHAPTER SIX

Keeping Going: the morale of local institutions

The morale of the civilian population depended on all residents giving each other support and care and on the spirit of defiance that might be engendered by parties, social occasions of a more formal kind, amateur dramatics, and patriotic celebrations. Several groups were disbanded. In 1942 the Petersham Young People's club closed for lack of members due to call-up, and earlier the Petersham Horticultural Show held a special General Meeting to consider disbanding for the duration of the war. But in general the existing churches, schools and clubs provided the principal lifelines, because public facilities were few and popular entertainment of a commercial character was not profitable in small communities. There was no public library in Ham or Petersham. Borrowing a good book required a journey into Richmond Library. Going to see a good film at the cinema or to see a play at the Richmond Theatre or Kingston Empire similarly meant taking the bus. Cinemas were closed on Sundays until 1944, when only those over 16 were then allowed in.

Churches

At *St. Peter's*, Petersham, on the outbreak of war it was decided that the Parochial clubs and fellowships would go ahead with their winter plans. At the end of 1939 the Church was badly hit by the call-up of key members of the congregation: both the organist and his deputy were called away for war work, and therefore experiments were made with a piano for when organists were unavailable. Vancouver celebration services were held in 1939 and 1940, with the latter on a larger scale, attended by 14 Canadians, including 2 from Vancouver, and was broadcast to Canada, but in 1941 and 1942 there were only private wreath-laying ceremonies. 1944 was, however, the 135th anniversary of the burial of George Vancouver; it was celebrated quietly. No service was held in 1945, but it was hoped to resume them the following year. The Village Hall, of course, was out of action due to the radar research, as was the Vicarage and All Saints'. There was severe bomb damage to the Church in November 1940 that cost £39 to put right, and in November 1943 further damage was caused. Mrs Warde of Petersham House hosted Parish parties and garden fetes; in 1941 she invited Caledonian pipers to provide music, and the garden fete in 1945 raised £100. In 1940 railings in the churchyard produced 10 tons of metal for the War effort.

At *St Andrew's* (also known as Ham parish church), in common with most churches, the evening services were changed from 6.30 to 5.45pm because of the blackout, but reverted to the normal time during the summer. In 1939 the Christmas Fair was abandoned, but the Mothers' Union provided a pantomime. Collections of clothes were made for the homeless, and a Jumble Sale mounted in 1940 to swell the total. Two stirrup pumps were purchased in 1940, and training given to volunteers on how to use them. The choir continued to function; choirboys were taken to the pantomimes, including *Aladdin* at Richmond Theatre and at Kingston Empire in 1941, and *Cinderella* at Kingston Empire. On a more serious note, the boys joined with the Tiffin School Band in a marquee on Richmond Green in aid of the Mayor's Victory Thanksgiving Fund. One year, a choirboy came first in the solo section of the Kingston Music Festival. Activities for both old and young continued: Youth Fellowship, Girls' Club, a Football Club for the boys that competed in league and cup matches, Women's Fellowship and Mothers' Union.

Outside activities for the Women's Fellowship and Mothers' Union included a river trip ending with tea at Sunbury Court (59 attended), a Mothers' Union trip to Croydon for a diocesan festival and a Women's Fellowship whist drive in aid of the boiler fund they also had a hike to Box Hill in 1943

The Church celebrated its 112th anniversary in October 1943; earlier that year it had marked the 4th anniversary of the outbreak of War. A record number of communicants was recorded in 1944. This followed confirmation of 60 by the Bishop.

There were a few problems: a window was blown out by a severe gale that caused damage to local trees, but this was not put right until after the end of hostilities, by which time there had been bomb blast damage to several other windows, which was not put right until after the end of hostilities; by that time there had been bomb blast damage to several other windows. In 1943 the green velvet curtains behind the children's altar were stolen, and may have ended up as smart dresses for keen sewing machine users. The choirboys' cassocks wore out by 1943, and the Vicar appealed, not for funds for their replacement, but for clothing coupons. A junior branch of the Girls' Club was formed in 1943. In January that year the Boys' and Girls' Clubs held a joint social event at the Ham Institute, despite an air-raid warning, but the following year the summer fete was abandoned because of the danger of V2 rockets; the alternative Gift Day, however, raised twice as much as usual.

At Christmas 1944 there was a foretaste of many current TV programmes. Leaflets were provided to the congregation asking them for their favourite carols; *Silent Night* came top, followed by *It came upon the midnight clear*. More than one vote was cast for carols with music by Peter Warlock and Vaughan Williams, but *Good King Wenceslas* obtained only one vote!

At *Ham Free Church* services continued throughout the war, with the usual adjustment of evening worship times because of the blackout. 1943 saw the 15th anniversary celebrations. In 1944 there was a special service of carols and Christmas music, where congre-gations from Cranford, Hounslow and Mitcham Lane joined the Ham worshippers.

Ham Institute in New Road served as the Hall of St Andrew's Church, but was used widely for other purposes. It had a mem-bership outside of the Church, and ran monthly socials comprising such things as games, competitions and entertainments, dances attracting up to 150 people. It was also used for fund-raising events, and even a lecture on the history of Austria following the First World War, though the attendance figures for this are not known!

Schools

The management of local schools was an important element in the maintenance of good civilian morale. As in the discussions on the Grey Court nursery school, parents were anxious to ensure that the war did not damage their children's education.

At the *Russell School* in Petersham trenches were dug in the Park near the School in 1939, accommodating 60 out of the 70 pupils and open to all ouside of school hours. We must assume that the remaining lived nearby, but ultimately there was no problem as pupil numbers had plunged to 30 by 1943. These excavations struck the water pipe taking the stream from the Park, and the school had to be housed temporarily in the crypt of All Saints' before the radar teams moved in. The first prize-giving since the war was held in 1942; it was announced that 4-year-olds would be admitted from the Autumn, and that hot meals would be provided for the 61 pupils. In 1943 it was announced that during the previous 13 years every pupil had qualified for secondary or central school, and that the meals provided had created considerable improvements in the weight and general condition of the pupils. When tragedy struck at 10.45pm on 8 November 1943 with the destruction of the School by two 500lb high explosive bombs, a move was made to Trefoil House, where it remained for the rest of the War and continued for. years afterwards. An application was made for the use of Petersham

House (also affected by bombing), but the Council decided that the cost of such a move would incur too great expense for toilet facilities, and that they could not imagine a less suitable place for the School. A request was made for permission to rebuild on the old site, but the Ministry of Education refused this on the grounds that circumstances had changed, and there were to be no more buildings erected in the Park. Even the request for compensation was fought against on the grounds that the School had been paying nothing for the site, except for a small annual sum to Surrey County Council. Eventually £350 was granted. When the School celebrated Empire Day in 1945, with the Mayoress present, an Australian Army sergeant gave a short talk.

The *Ham Schools* (in the building now housing St Thomas Aquinas Church) were Church of England, connected to St. Andrew's. Air raid protection in the early days of the War was by the use of trenches dug on Ham Common. These would accommodate only 90 of the 276 pupils at the school. It was considered that the majority of children were within five minutes' walk of their homes, where shelter would be available. The trenches on the Common were of a different pattern to those in Petersham, less deep and banked up at the top because of problems with the water table. By the middle of 1942 the school had collected over 9 tons of waste paper. After the war the Wardens' post attached to the School was incorporated for a maximum of 5 years. The sports days were held on the Common. The Schools collected paper, rags, books and magazines to raise funds for the Services. At the end of the War the new Parochial Church Council appointed Mrs Lionel Warde of Petersham as its Manager.

There was no provision for secondary education in Ham and Petersham; so all older children were forced to travel into Richmond each school day. Two bus routes served them: the 65, which ran quite frequently, and the 73, twice an hour. Those buses had netting attached to the inside of all windows, with a diamond-shaped, wood-surrounded area of clear glass to allow passengers a limited vision. Fuelled by petrol, with open platforms, their seating capacity during the morning and evening was used by local children travelling largely against the stream of workers aiming for the Kingston factories. There were bus shelters at the Common and Sandy Lane, but the Petersham children had no such shelter.

Meals were not provided at school, but free bus tickets were given to children to allow them to get home and back at lunchtime.

Early in 1940 150 mothers petitioned for better school transport.

Richmond asked the London Transport Board to provide extra buses, and the results of a survey carried out at Sandy Lane on 24 January 1940 indicated that sufficient were available between the hours of 7.59 and 8.59, with the following result:

Total number of buses arriving: 17 (mostly on the 65 route)

8.09am 15 passengers were left behind, including 6 children

8.14am 6 children were still at the stop, but 2 minutes later another bus cleared the queue.

Sandy Lane in 1938, looking towards main road. (David Williams' collection)

From that point on, there was no further problem reported. These results were printed in the Council minutes, and no future survey was recorded. However, the problem continued. In 1942 Councillor Allum said he had seen three children waiting from 8.30 to 9.15am for their bus, following the proposed alteration of Richmond school opening hours from 9.30 to 9am. It appeared that our local children were being crowded off the buses.

The principal clubs and societies

There were a number of local clubs which were set up before the amalgamation of Ham and Petersham. Their war-time impro-visations provided many opportunities for the residents to meet each other.

The *Petersham and Ham Women's Institute* founded in 1923, always combining the two villages after the amalgamation, remained active throughout the War, meeting monthly in Trefoil House. Its first thought was to carry on without speakers, whilst continuing its whist drives, but in the end it continued with various social activities, supported by as many as 100 people. It celebrated its 18th birthday at Ham Farm in 1941, which takes its origins back to the time before Ham became incorporated into Richmond. Singing was an important part of its activities: members joined in community singing at a social following a visit to Kew Gardens in 1941, and its own choir sang in the Reigate Festival in 1942. In 1944 the choir took part in the music festival of the Surrey Festival of Women's Institutes, conducted by Ralph Vaughan Williams. WI speakers included the first woman Mayor of Richmond in 1942 and one on the design of prefabricated houses at its 21st anniversary meeting. In 1941 it held the first of a series of demonstrations of wartime cookery at Trefoil House. Its 20th anniversary in 1943 was celebrated with soldiers as guests and later in the year a party was held at Trefoil House for 20 ex-servicemen from the Star and Garter Home; this included a whist drive, games, competitions, community singing and drama. The click of knitting needles was heard regularly in aid of good causes, and for sending to the Royal Corps of Signals (123 garments) and the Merchant Navy (70 garments).

The *Petersham and Ham Sea Scouts* had an even longer history than the Womens' Institute. Founded in 1908, it was one of the oldest such troops in the world, celebrating their 54th anniversary in 1942. They were very active on several fronts during the War with a membership at times of over 150. They supported the War efforts by helping the National Fire Service, local Fire Guards, Home Guard and Civil Defence, and by assisting in the salvage drive and erecting Morrison shelters in homes. By 1944 they had 125 ex-members serving in the armed forces; three of this number had been killed on active service. In 1944 the Admiralty inspecting officer said that comments were made all over the country about Petersham's excellence.

They had a strong sporting and social aspect. In 1941 there was the annual cross-country championship and the swimming gala; in 1942 a signalling contest and a competitive 60-mile cycle marathon in which their A team came first and their B team second. The following year they came second in the camp craft competition. Their football team was fairly successful, beating East Sheen in 1944, and in 1945 winning six out of their 10 matches. Socials were held, including at least one organised by the Air Arm section, formed in 1943. At their 1942 Christmas party, Guides were entertained with radiogram, games and singing; 200 people were present on that occasion. In 1945 their Social was held at the Institute, with games, dancing and competition. It was reported that more of the boys were dancing, after classes at their HQ.

Properly, not all their activities were land-based. A regatta with a 4-hour programme was held in 1942, and they were involved in more than one rescue from the Thames, and in 1942 a Rover Scout was awarded a medal for one such incident. We can be proud of their achievements, which were not only observed by Ham and Petersham. In 1942 they gave a display on Richmond Green, pre-ceded by a march through the town with their colours, accompanied by the band. In 1943 their newly re-formed Air Arm section assisted in Kingston's 'Wings for Victory' campaign, raising £60.

Every year the Troop set up camp at Thorpe Farm near Virginia Water, or in 1943 to Chalfont Heights in Chalfont St Peter, where they gave assistance to the local farmers, travelling by river and camping overnight if necessary. Eventually a permanent camping site was acquired at Hemsworth, near Chichester.

The *Ham and Petersham Rifle Club* was even older than the Sea Scouts. It had been founded in 1906 'in order to strengthen the de-fences of this country'. It remained active at the beginning of War so that the Army would not be tempted to take over their range. In 1942 members of the Boys' Club were receiving training in firing rifles. In 1943 a Scouts Rifle Club was formed. Air Raid Wardens were given training here, according to Marjorie Lansdale. In 1945 it won the open team event for Salisbury Challenge Cup in Surrey Rifle Association victory programme with an average score of 96.5.

The *Ham and Petersham Cricket Club* can date its origins to the matches played on Ham Common in the early nineteen century. Its present name has been used since 1891. A club for 14-year-olds was planned at the AGM in 1940. The Army Radio School cricket team (consisting entirely of officers) beat the Hounslow HQ team and lost only one of four reported matches, including those against Richmond and the REME school teams. The *Petersham Sports and Social Club* suspended its activities during the war, partly because of the presence of the radio school.

Richmond Golf Club: Founded in 1891, it occupied the Palladian mansion of Sudbrook House and its grounds. It was active through-out the War, and in 1940 imposed temporary rules as follows:

(1) Players are asked to collect Bomb and Shrapnel splinters to save these causing damage to the Mowing Machines.

(2) In competitions, during gunfire or while bombs are falling, players may take cover without penalty for ceasing play.

(3) The position of known delayed action bombs are marked by red flags at a reasonably, but not guaranteed, safe distance therefrom.

(4) Shrapnel and/or bomb splinters on the Fairways, or in Bunkers within a club's length of a ball, may be moved without penalty, and no penalty shall be if a ball is caused to be moved accidentally.

(5) A ball moved by enemy action may be replaced, and if lost or destroyed, a ball may be dropped not nearer the hole without penalty.

(6) A ball lying in a crater may be lifted and dropped not nearer the hole, preserving the line to the hole, without penalty.

(7) A player whose stroke is affected by the simultaneous explosion of a bomb may play another ball from the same place. Penalty: one stroke.

It is reported that Dr Goebbels announced on the German radio: 'By means of these ridiculous reforms, the English snobs try to impress the people with a kind of pretend heroism. They can do so without danger, because, as everyone knows, the German Air Force devotes itself only to the destruction of military targets and objectives of importance to the war effort.'

Some such rules were needed: at least two high explosive bombs, a 'bread basket' and a V1 flying bomb were recorded.

General social activities. There were several amateur dramatic productions, but apart from the WI choir and church choirs no local singing group. A fortnightly discussion group was formed in Stretton Road in 1942. Music for dances was provided by several groups including Duggie Dean's Night Owls; police entertainment groups also enlivened several functions. At home there were only two UK radio programmes, the Home and the Light programmes; they provided more varied fare than the rather compartmentalised ones we are now used to. The record player or radiogram was also available, some with wind-up mechanism, and probably most using steel needles. It was possible to receive foreign radio stations, particularly Radio Luxemburg (for popular music) or the broadcasts from Germany of Lord Haw Haw (William Joyce, whose rantings caused many laughs, as well as disquiet for the nervous). The blackout did not inhibit people from going out at nights for dances, whist drives, lectures and social events that would include games and competitions. The Ham and Petersham Young People's Club decided early in the War to go ahead with 'dramatics, but not whist drives or dances', but hoped to run lantern lectures and social evenings. The Mothers' Union produced a pantomime and continued their annual dance. The Stretcher Party and Ham Fire Guards ran socials. There were gymkhanas on Ham Common run by the Home Guard. Knitting parties, in addition to that of the WI, existed: at St Andrew's and through the Womens' Conservative Association; Mrs Kinton lent her shop on Ham Parade for the sale of knitted items.

In 1940 Mead Road staged a street party where children gave a concert in Mr Bennett's garden, a dolls' name-guessing competition with eggs and a rabbit as prizes to raise money for prisoners of war. Carpets and chairs were ranged across the road, flags unearthed for decorations, and even the air raid shelter decorated. The door of the road's bombed house was used as an improvised platform. The Mayor attended, and praised the residents' efforts.

Dramatic productions included *Nine till Six* that was also performed at Richmond's Castle Hotel in 1944, and the Girls' Club adaptation of *Gone with the Wind*.

The Ratepayers' Association

The function of the Ham and Petersham Ratepayers' Association was not to create social occasions, but to continue providing a voice for local opinion on planning matters, such as those raised by Richmond Council. In 1939 it was hard hit by the call-up, but decided to carry on, even if its usefulness and extent of powers was undecided. It showed confidence in a British victory just before the outbreak of war, when the Association, faced with the removal of the First World War's German gun on Ham Common, asked that it should be replaced by its modern equivalent when victory was secured. This did not happen, but nobody appeared to have bothered. Perhaps it would have reminded too many people of lost sleep through anti-aircraft fire.

Also just before the outbreak of War it had pressed for the opening of a second Post Office and provision of extra stamp machines. At the 1940 AGM there were complaints that not enough information was being passed on by the three Councillors, and by 1941 there had been a fall in the association's membership, though 119 subscriptions had been received. The Chairman, Major McGrath, said that Councillor Westlake 'had shown that a Petersham resident could look after the interests of Ham ... he had fought the scheme for a refuse dump'. This proposal was refused in 1940 by Buckminster Estates on the grounds that the Defence Regulations did not allow this; it was suggested that help could be sought from Kingston instead. The 1942 AGM criticised the cost of the 'Holidays at Home' scheme that encouraged holidaymakers to avoid travelling any distance (all overseas holidays, of course, being out of the question). It pointed out that the crowds produced made it almost impossible to travel from Richmond and Petersham on a Sunday.

But on more serious matters it continued performing a real service to the community. It fought against the proposal to site the Surrey County Council sewage works on Ham Lands. This provoked local fury and the association made a house-to-house survey to find out what residents' views were.

It objected to proposals to allow extension of the factory buildings within the Ham River Grit Company's area. In 1942 that company applied for permission to build an extension to their workshop; this would occupy a 2-acre site, but the Company could provide no confirmation that its production would be directly for the War effort. The Ratepayers' Association objected, and this plan for building was eventually rejected by the Council in April 1943 after its initial agreement. An appeal from the Company was refused again, though the appeal was supported by the Ministry of Supply, Who were happy for the building to remain until 1948. Eventually a Local Enquiry was held on 13 July 1943. The plan was modified to allow removal of the whole building within 6 months of victory. In 1945 an application for a year-by-year extension of the concrete casting work on Ham Lands was finally turned down, but 1 years grace allowed instead of previous 6 months was agreed. and in 1944 circulated reminders of potential post-war developments to all houses in the Ward. At the 1945 AGM the Mayor (a Sudbrook councillor) answered questions on this last subject. It was responsible for choosing the new Councillor when one of the three resigned. And there was at least one fund-raising effort, in the form of a dance. When post-war plans for building were formulated, it suggested that the density should be 12 to the acre between Sandy Lane and River Lane, but the Council decided only 8.

In 1943 Richmond Council agreed in principle 'the development and improvement of Ham Pond', to 'make site more pleasant as a place for exercise and recreation.' The Ratepayers' Association must have put forward their view on this, and the following year the Vice-Chairman of the Georgian Group wrote to the *Richmond and Twickenham Times* regarding this proposal to 'improve' Ham Pond: 'In the midst of a terrible war the RBC proposes plans for altering the outline of a charming pond. Not only is the shape of the pond to be changed to an ellipse with a kerb and concrete edging of great width, but the layout is to be "suitably ornamented".'

Everybody faced one basic problem. With the onset of War, building materials were not readily obtainable, except for bomb damage repairs. This is borne out by the decision of Richmond Council in 1943 to repaint 85 Council houses externally, as enough paint was being released. They did, however, manage to make up the roads on the latest section of the Ham Estate. Early in the War the *Fox & Duck* public house was demolished and rebuilt; there were complaints that the materials could have been used better elsewhere.

The old Fox & Duck before demolition. (David Williams' collection)

John Randle VC

John Randle when he lost his life was 26 years old and a Temporary Captain in the 2nd Battalion, the Royal Norfolk Regiment. Captain Randle was commander of 'B' Company of the Royal Norfolk Regiment. On 4 May 1944 during the Battle of Kohima in North East India he was ordered to attack the Japanese flank on GPT Ridge during the relief and clearance of Kohima. The citation from the *London Gazette* reads:

On the 4th May, 1944, at Kohima in Assam, a Battalion of the Norfolk Regiment attacked the Japanese positions on a nearby ridge. Captain Randle took over command of the Company which was leading the attack when the Company Commander was severely wounded. His handling of a difficult situation in the face of heavy fire was masterly and although wounded himself in the knee by grenade splinters he continued to inspire his men by his initiative, courage and outstanding leadership until the Company had captured its objective and consolidated its position. He then went forward and brought in all the wounded men who were lying outside the perimeter. In spite of his painful wound Captain Randle refused to be evacuated and insisted on carrying out a personal reconnaissance with great daring in bright moonlight prior to a further attack by his Company on the position to which the enemy had withdrawn. At dawn on 6th May the attack opened, led by Captain Randle, and one of the platoons succeeded in reaching the crest of the hill held by the Japanese. Another platoon, however, ran into heavy medium machine gun fire from a bunker on the reverse slope of the feature.

Captain Randle immediately appreciated that this particular bunker covered not only the rear of his new position but also the line of communication of the battalion and therefore the destruction of the enemy post was imperative if the operation was to succeed. With utter disregard of the obvious danger to himself Captain Randle charged the Japanese machine gun post single-handed with rifle and bayonet. Although bleeding in the face and mortally wounded by numerous busts of machine gun fire he reached the bunker and silenced the gun with a grenade

John Randle
(Photograph
courtesy
of his son)

thrown through the bunker slit. He then flung his body across the slit so that the aperture should be completely sealed. The bravery shown by this officer could not have been surpassed and by his self-sacrifice he saved the lives of many of his men and enabled not only his own Company but the whole Battalion to gain its objective and win a decisive victory over the enemy.

A memorial to John Randle can be seen inside St Peter's Church. After the War the Council decided to name a new road (off Craig Road) after him – a rare distinction at the time, although later several of the blocks of flats in Ham Close were named after his contemporaries. In fact, the family did not live in Ham or Petersham, but occupied a house in Queen's Road, Richmond, near the Star and Garter Home. But the naming of the road in Ham after the only VC in Richmond borough makes him of particular local importance; he is also commemorated in Norwich in the same way because of his service (one of five VCs in the regiment) with the Norfolks.

The black marble memorial, next to the Vancouver memorial, is of fine quality, with lettering and regimental crest prepared and executed by The Craftsmens Guild, of the Oval, SE11.

CHAPTER SEVEN

Victory and reconstruction

With the end of the War, blackout restrictions all gone, house building to resume and servicemen about to return from their duties, street lighting to be restored by the end of double summer time, it was time for celebrating. Food was to be rationed for some years to come (some rations were actually cut soon afterwards), but enough could be found to feed the street parties that were held. All war damage was to be put right by mid-1945; salvage was still collected, and none of it was allowed to be used for celebratory bonfires. The public shelters were closed, but there was no labour available to remove the Anderson shelters; if householders removed them the metal had to be retained safely. They could be bought for £1, and the Morrison shelters (for which no labour was available for quick removal) could be bought for £1.10s.

Mead and Craig Roads held their party at the Ham Institute; there was also a street celebration attended by the Mayor and Mayoress with tea, bonfire and fireworks Lawrence Road and Langham Gardens combined for theirs, as did Mowbray, Ashburnham and Sheridan Roads. Broughton Avenue hired a Punch & Judy show, and had toddlers' fancy dress competition; they also had community singing accompanied by accordion and double bass; the cost was 1s. each plus a 1s. savings stamp. A party was held at the *Fox & Duck*, with the Mayor and Mayoress in attendance (they also attended some of the street parties). A WI party with entertainment was held at Langham House Hotel. The Park Estate (Sandy Lane etc.) went for something grander, with theirs at Matthies restaurant in Kew Road.

Street lighting was restored when double summer time ended though the fuel shortage did not allow for them all to be lit. All bomb damage had been put right by midsummer. Permission for a bonfire was refused, though later there was one for VJ day. There were no collections taken at Victory church services. Removal of wooden covers and ramps of shelters were to be removed, but Richmond said there was no labour available for this and suggested using prisoners of war instead.

With the advent of the V1 flying bombs, the blackout was to be lifted in 1944, and ARP precautions ended in daylight. Ice cream, however, remained discontinued and fuel rationing remained in force. The same year two councillors expressed the view that rate-controlled housing should not be given to those with cars. A study of ex-council houses locally will show how few even now have garages, unless there is space for one in the garden. The Highways Committee suggested in June 1944 the construction of a loop line between Richmond and Kingston, additional buses and the safeguarding of Petersham Village from through traffic.

Local heroes

John Randle (see pp. 57-8) was the most celebrated local hero. There were others, and of course those who lost their lives. A British Empire Medal was awarded to a seaman from Mowbray Road in 1944; in the same year a Distinguished Flying Cross awarded to a local squadron-leader and a Military Cross to a resident of Sudbrook Gardens. In December a Distinguished Flying Cross was awarded to a resident of Sudbrook Gardens, who was killed in a landing accident soon afterwards. The names of those killed in air raids, where known, are listed above. The war memorial in Ham records the names of 42 service personnel and 8 civilians killed during the War. The Petersham memorial has only 10 names, reflecting the difference in population.

Local politics

Victory also stimulated thoughts about post-war reconstruction. The questions raised by the Ham town planning scheme in 1937 returned to the local political agenda. What kind of development was to be judged appropriate for the area? What kinds of facilities should be provided?

Towards a Plan for Richmond was published by its Council in 1945. A Reconstruction Office was to be set up, but for the open lands at Ham, plans had already been made before the War. The emphasis for our locality was on traffic planning, with a Petersham Bypass, crossing Petersham Park, skirting the built-up edge of Petersham and rejoining the main road by a roundabout at Sandy Lane. The sop to the many households who had no car was a proposal for a greatly improved bus service; for visitors, car parks were planned for Ham Lands and Petersham Meadows. A strip of open land ¼ mile wide was to adjoin the river. Four Nursery Schools, 2 Infant, 2 Junior and 1 'modern' were to be established.

But if the initiative lay largely with Richmond Council, the Ratepayers' Association, formed in 1933, still played a part in monitoring unsuitable local developments. The full revival of its activities in 1948-9 quickly lost momentum in spite of attempts to broaden its appeal. In 1950 it became the 'Ham and Petersham Ratepayers and Residents Association', thus opening its membership to council house tenants. There had been no local elections during the War. Sudbrook Ward had three Councillors, but only one had been chosen by local people, the other two having been transferred from the old South Ward, as was the successful candidate in 1933, Alfred Allum, the steward to Lionel Warde of Petersham House, who joined Councillors Walters and Westlake (later, in 1944, Mayor), both of whom were very active subsequently in Ham and Petersham. When Councillor Walters resigned in 1941 and it became necessary to replace him, the Ratepayers' Association was asked to nominate the successor. They chose Mr W. A. Thompson of Sheridan Road, a member of the Association since its inception and had shown much interest in local affairs, particularly sport; he offered to supply 2–3,000 plants for the new Nursery School, and became a regular attendant at Council meetings, serving on the Health, Housing and Rights of Way & Surveyor's committees. 1n 1944 he became a Conservator of Petersham Common, and was on the Allotments committee. Despite his sterling work for the area, he came bottom of the poll when local elections were resumed in 1945. Not everybody was happy with the proposal to nominate Mr Thompson. Two other names were put forward locally: Mr S. L. Brown was a strong candidate, but an excuse was put forward that due to the 'blitz' it was not possible to have any kind of local contest; his name would be put forward next time, however, he did not stand in 1945. The vote of the Ratepayers' Association was strongly in favour of Mr Thompson, who declared that he would fight for the rights of Council tenants.

Richmond's Conservative MP, George Harvie-Watt, who won the by-election in 1937, became PPS to Winston Churchill in 1941. He secured re-election in 1945 with a majority over his Labour opponent (Dr Stark Murray – a student of law); the Liberal (Major Douglas Gordon) and Common Wealth (Douglas Frank) candidates lost their deposits. He never appears in any newspaper reports relating to Ham, but was quite active in Conservative functions held in Petersham. An unfortunate incident occurred in 1942 at their open-air meeting at Montrose House, when reporters from the *Daily Herald* and *Reynolds News* claimed that remarks (actually made by another man) sneered that 'those who advocated the Second Front (a continual request of Stalin) 'had never distinguished themselves by any great desire to shoulder arms'. He won a libel action against the papers, which retracted the allegation. The remark, however, seems to have been picked up by German radio.

For Richmond Council the immediate future was largely occupied with housing, not with additions to local facilities. The current housing list was closed, and a system of points evolved to give the order of priority, as follows:

If bombed out, 5 points
For each year of residence prior to 1935–, ¼ point
Each member of family, 1 point
If in lodgings, 5 points
If rent more than one-fifth of income, 2 points
If living in overcrowded or insanitary condition, 10 points
For each year of service in Forces, 1 point
Priority was to be given to tuberculosis cases.
Later an extra 3 points added if applicant employed in Richmond.

The quickest solution to the housing demand was by use of mainly imported prefabricated bungalows. These were of Archon Mark V design, not the cheapest, as they provided a separate hallway. The sites earmarked for them were a major development of 100 on what is now Ham Close, and sites at Latchmere Lane and Back Lane. The rent was fixed at 10s per week. There was some dispute with Kingston over the Latchmere Lane site, earmarked for 103 houses; Kingston claimed that the site was too isolated from Richmond, and had deficient access for services. They wanted half the site for playgrounds, but Richmond refused, and the dispute went to the Ministry of Housing. In the end Kingston was allocated 9.49 acres, Richmond only 5.94.

Plans were already made for permanent housing, on the following basis: Two-thirds were to be of 3 bedrooms, and the 32 houses for the Murray/Stretton/Neville Road sites; 116 for Back Lane site, later rescinded in favour of use for community purposes (we must remember that at the time Back Lane ran as far as what is now Wiggins Lane); 72 flats in Hardwicke Road and the acquisition, after a public enquiry, of the Hawker sports field and other open land between that and the Lock footpath to provide 800 dwellings, thus helping to reduce the current waiting list of 1064.. These would match the standard of pre-war developments, and work began with the help of prisoner-of-war labour. The 8.06 acres already earmarked for housing and 1.88 designated for recreation should be used for 'working class' housing only. The 15.74 acres between the Common and Sandy Lane should be acquired for educational and recreational purposes – much of this is now Grey Court School, though a correspondent to the local Press thought that these should also be built on, believing this would happen sooner or later. At this point Park Road was renamed Ham Gate 'Road' later changed to

'Avenue' rather more appropriately.

Ham and Petersham did not acquire the assets from government war-time investment which some other places enjoyed. Towns as different from each other as Newcastle-upon-Tyne and Harrogate retained many of the public sector jobs which had arisen from the evacuation of government departments. Stanstead and Castle Donington had air force aerodromes that could be converted into major airports. Malvern, not Petersham, benefitted from radar research. The relocation in 1942 of both the Air Defence Research and Development Establishment and the Telecommunications Research Establishment to Malvern gave the town not only a source of employment but also subsidies from government to cover the cost of council housing. The property commandeered in Petersham was never likely to remain in public hands. In 1946 when the Army Operational Research Group based in Petersham moved to West Byfleet, that village became the beneficiary of Petersham's war-time deprivations.

An artistic event with local connections was a National Gallery exhibition that included a whole room devoted to paintings of Ham and Petersham, selected because they were 'full of beautiful 17th-century houses and because their nearness to London makes survival in their present state as doubtful tomorrow as it is surprising today'. We are grateful that this was a mistaken view; thanks to local pressure the character of Petersham in particular has been maintained..

By the end of the war Ham and Petersham had been united for twelve years—six in peace and six in war. Regarded since 1935 as parts of the London Green Belt, both villages came within the purview of post-war planning for Greater London. The *Greater London Plan* of 1944 commissioned by the Ministry of Works in 1942 from Sir Patrick Abercrombie covered many such suburban sites. Questions about their future development were entangled in the discussion of bigger problems such as the design of road systems and the need for 'overspill' housing. The Abercrombie plan suggested that Ham House should be acquired by the nation and used as a museum and picture gallery.

At that mansion all its social activities had ceased for some years. Its owner, Sir Lyonel Tollemache, the 4th Baronet (1854–1952) and the second cousin and heir of the 9th Earl of Dysart (1859–1935), was 85 when the War began, though he still took enough interest in those whose leases were held by him. He was concerned that such title deeds should be kept safe; it had been suggested that they be stored in Ham House itself, but he preferred that they should go to the Public Records Office in Chancery Lane. Here they came to grief when incendiary bombs set fire to it; the documents were not burned, but were destroyed by the water that was intended to save them. In March 1943 he received a visit from the National Trust buildings adviser, James Lees-Milne, who wished to consider the possibility of the house being taken into the Trust's ownership. He wrote in his report: 'the grounds are indescribably overgrown and unkempt. I passed long ranges of semi-derelict outhouses. The garden is pitted with bomb craters around the house, from which a few windows have been blown out and the busts from the niches torn away . . .There is no doubt whatsoever that even without the contents this house is worthy of acceptance because of the superlative interior treatment . . .' In 1948 Sir Lyonel and his son, Cecil (1886–1969), presented the house to the Trust, but its contents under a separate set of negotiations were purchased by the government and taken into the care of the Victoria & Albert Museum. The house and contents were on a lease administered by the Ministry of Works.

The decision of the National Trust to take over Ham House and the land around it emphasised the importance in local politics of the need to continue protecting the landscape of the Thames valley and the view from Richmond Hill. The future of the Ham Lands and of the shape of Ham as part of a new suburb for Richmond remained subjects that aroused emotion. The unfinished business of the Ham town planning scheme of 1937 came to dominate the agenda of the future.

THE END: A victory party at the Hawker Sports & Social Club
(photograph supplied by Gill Douglas-Smith)

APPENDIX

Where the bombs fell

Information concerning the amount of damage caused is limited, as local newspapers were forbidden to give such details. Early in the war photographs of damage were published, but no clue given as to the area affected. It was not very long before none at all were shown. Personal reminiscences have provided some information, and a little can be gleaned from Council reports of grants for repair. Although the list is not long, the bombing was no less intense that other parts of outer London; it is disguised by the number of them that fell on open ground and did no damage to houses. A diary kept by a local schoolboy from 22 November 1940 to the end of that year has provided useful information, not least with timings and intensity of anti-aircraft fire, which, with more than one alert period during some nights, must have made sleep difficult. Records show that the following houses were destroyed or badly damaged: established, the following roads were affected by bomb damage:
(HE = high explosive bomb, In. = incendiary bomb)
Arlington Road. HE on No.12 1.10.40; In. on 6, 7, 8 & 19 16.11.40.
Ashley Gardens. In. on 6 & 8, 16.11.40.
The Avenue, Ham Common. HE on 20.11.40; In. near Sandy Lane 16.11.40; HE between Sandy Land & Ham House 19.2.41.
Broughton Avenue. HE on No. 5 on 9.10.40; Nos. 9 & 11 on 23.10.40.
Bute Avenue. Mr & Mrs Naylor (he a part-time Air Raid Warden) killed 9 .11.40. *Quaint Cottage.* HE 10.10.40.
Church Road. HEs on 26.9.40 and 29.11.40. Land-mine scored a direct hit on Latchmere detention centre; a stick of bombs fell in grounds. *Wilmer & Equestrian Club.* Four HE and In. on 24.2.41
Craig Road. Nos. 2–8 on 30.11.40; included in the compulsory purchase order (see *Lock Road*).
Dukes Avenue. HE on 156-8 29.11.40: a flying bomb caused considerable damage when it fell in Dysart Avenue in 1944.
Golf Club. HE (unexploded) on 16.9.40; HE on 10th green 26.9.40; HE (unexploded) 29.11.40; V1 flying bomb 20.8.44.
Ham Common. In. 26.9.40 & 1.10.40 (15–20). HE 9.10.40 and 20.11.40. 2 V1 flying bombs fell on the boundary with the Golf Course. Flying bomb fell in grounds of Lawrence Hall Hotel (now the Cassel Hospital). *Endsleigh Lodge.* A bomb hit a tree in the garden, did not damage the house. *Eckett & Ellis's yard.* In., 1.10.40. (See below for Mr Adams's garage.) HE on Oak Lodge 29.11.40.

Official record says this did not explode, but Marjorie Lansdale (*Reminiscences*) writes that family of four was killed at dinner.

Ham Fields. 5 HE (3 unexploded) 24.9.40; 2 HE opposite Eel Pie Island 24.9.40; In.10.10.40.

Ham House: HEs in grounds 1.10.40 and 9.11.40; In. in grounds 16.11.40.

Ham River Grit Co. 20–30 In. 1.10.40; 1 In. 10.10.40.

Ham Street. HE at Almshouses, 28.10.40 and on corner with Lock Road 20.11.40. HE at Kent's Nursery 13.2.41; In. at Manor House 16.11.40.

Langham House & Lawrence Hall Hotel: 'Breadbasket' of incendiaries fell 1.10.40.

Lawrence Road. Nos. 36–50, on 30 November 1940.

Lock Road. HE on corner with Ham Street 20.11.40; considerable damage: Nos. 25–46 on 29 November 1940, but no casualties. That site was compulsorily purchased by the Council for £405, rebuilt after the War and now has a gap in the house numbering. A static water tank was put on the site. HE on No.15 20.11.40.

Mead Road. Two HE 23.11.40; 1 person killed; HE on No. 29 20.11.40

Mowbray Road. 5 houses destroyed in 1944.

New Road. Nos. 38–47 on 29.11.40; part of the site was used for erecting a Wardens' Hut, after requisitioning by Council.

Orford House (now St Michaels' Convent). Damage caused to greenhouses at rear of house.

Petersham & Ham Sea Scouts: In. in Douglas Meadow 29.11.40.

Petersham Park: HE on 9.11.40. 2 HEs east of *All Saints'* 10.11.40; HE S.E. of Church same night. Unexploded HE N. of ARP post 14.10.40.

Petersham Meadow: V1 flying bomb on 27.6.44.

Petersham Road. HE on 26.9.40; *The Copse*: In. on 16.11.40; *Douglas House*: HE on 26.9.40; *Dysart Arms*: HE on 29.11.40; *Elm* Lodge: HE on 29.11.40; HE opposite *Fox & Duck* 9.11.40; HE on *Oak Lodge* 29.11.40. Official record says this did not explode, but Marjorie Lansdale (*Reminiscences*) writes that family of four was killed at dinner. *The Old House*: In. on 23.11.40; *Petersham House*: HE on lawn 9.11.40; 'Breadbasket' of In. 29.9.40.

River Lane: Petersham Lodge. Considerable damage caused.

Russell School. Destroyed by 2 HEs 8.1.43 while sited in Petersham Park.

St Andrew's Church. Blast damage to windows and roof from the bomb on Mr Adams's garage (see below).

St Peter's Church. Damage sustained on two occasions.

Sandpits Road: HE on *The Thatch* on 9.11.40; HE between road and Sandy Lane 9.11.40; *Fields* at head of road: In. 16.11.40

Sandy Lane: HE between road and Sandpits Road 9.11.40; In. at Sandy Lodge 16.11.40; HEs at corner of Petersham Road and at Holly Walk 19.2.41.

Scarlett's Farm. 6 HE 28.10.40 (on farmland); 1 on barn same night.

Sea Scouts: In. in grounds 29.11.40.

Smardon's Fields: Four HEs on 9.11.40; In. 16.11.40.

Sudbrook Gardens. Incendiary bomb on Mulberry cottages 26.9.40.

Teddington Lock. Incendiary 19.10.40.

Mr Adams ran a garage on the east side of Ham Common, and also a small precision engineering works, called R&H Press Tools Ltd (so Marjorie Lansdale records) that made small parts for bombers and fighters, including the Mosquito. He was a well-known organist, holding at various times the posts of organist at St Peter's, Norbiton, the Regal cinema at Kingston and the Astoria cinema in the Old Kent Road. He also designed cinema organs at other places, and had his own pipe instrument on the site of the garage. In 1939 he had staged a local performance of *Messiah.* Garage, workshop and organ were destroyed by a direct hit; although the workshop carried on after repairs, the organ was lost.

The 460th Air Raid Warning was sounded in April 1941 (sometimes there were three in one day); that was the month of the heaviest raid of the War, though for Ham the worst days were 20 November 1940 and for Petersham 9 and 29 November 1940. From 1941 onwards there was only the occasional bomb recorded.

Mr Adams at the console of his organ. (Richmond Local Studies collection)

Bibliography

Blackett, P. M. S.: Studies of War: Nuclear and Conventional
(Oliver & Boyd, 1962)

Dobinson, Colin: Anti-Aircraft Command (Methuen, 2001)

Masterman, J. C.: The Double-cross System (Yale U.P., 1972)

Nye, Mary Jo: Blackett: physics, war and politics in the 20th
Century (Harvard U. P., 2004)

Pritchard, Evelyn: Ham House and its owners through five
centuries (Richmond Local History Society)

Pritchard, Evelyn (ed. Leonard Chave): Guide to the street names
of Ham and Petersham (Richmond Local History Society)

Richmond History *Richmond History* journal, particularly Nos. 26, 27,
28, 30.

Richmond Local History Society, for Ham Amenities Group:
Ham and Petersham at 2000 (ed. Leonard Chave)

Rowe, A. P.: One story of Radar (Cambridge U.P., 1948)

Stephens, R. W. G: Camp 020: MI5 and the Nazi Spies
(Bloomsbury Academic)

Walpole, Josephine: Vernon Ward, Child of the Edwardian
Era (Antique Collectors' Club 1988)

Index